DATE DUE

A YOUNG PEOPLE'S
HISTORY
of the UNITED STATES

VOLUME TWO

A YOUNG PEOPLE'S HISTORY *of the* UNITED STATES

VOLUME TWO

CLASS STRUGGLE *to the* WAR ON TERROR

HOWARD ZINN

Adapted by
REBECCA STEFOFF

SEVEN STORIES PRESS
New York · Toronto · London · Melbourne

A YOUNG PEOPLE'S HISTORY OF THE UNITED STATES
VOLUME II: CLASS STRUGGLE TO THE WAR ON TERROR

Howard Zinn
Adapted by Rebecca Stefoff

SEVEN STORIES PRESS
New York • Toronto • London • Melbourne

Copyright © 2007 by Howard Zinn

A Seven Stories Press First Edition

SEVEN STORIES PRESS
140 Watts Street, New York, NY 10013
www.sevenstories.com

College professors may order examination copies of
Seven Stories Press titles for a free six-month trial period.
To order, visit http://www.sevenstories.com/textbook
or send a fax on school letterhead to (212) 226-1411.

Library of Congress Cataloging-in-Publication Data
Stefoff, Rebecca, 1951-
A young people's history of the United States / Howard Zinn ; adapted by
Rebecca Stefoff.—Seven Stories Press 1st ed.
p. cm.
Includes bibliographical references and index.
ISBN: 978-1-58322-759-6 (paper over board : alk. paper)
ISBN: 978-1-58322-760-2 (paper over board : alk. paper)
1. United States—History—Juvenile literature.
I. Zinn, Howard, 1922- Young people's history of the United States. II. Title.
E178.3.S735 2007
973—dc22
2007008703

Design by Pollen, New York
Printed in the United States of America

5 6 7 8 9

Contents

To all the parents and teachers over the years who have asked for a people's history for young people, and to the younger generation, who we hope will use their talents to make a better world.

❖

Thanks to Dan Simon, of Seven Stories Press, for initiating this *Young People's History* and to Theresa Noll of Seven Stories Press, for steering the project so carefully through its various stages.

❖

A special appreciation to Rebecca Stefoff, who undertook the heroic job of adapting *A People's History* for young readers.

CHAPTER ONE

CLASS STRUGGLE

ANGER WAS ON THE RISE IN AMERICA AS the twentieth century opened. The United States had just won the Spanish-American War. Emma Goldman, an anarchist and feminist of the time, later remembered how the war in Cuba and the Philippines had filled people with patriotism:

> How our hearts burned with indignation against the atrocious Spaniards! . . . But when the smoke was over, the dead buried, and the cost of the war came back to the people in an increase in the price of commodities [goods] and rent—that is, when we sobered up from our patriotic spree—it suddenly dawned on us that the cause of the Spanish American war was the price of sugar . . . that the lives, blood and money of the American people were used to protect the interests of the American capitalists.

Some famous American writers spoke up for socialism, with harsh words for the capitalist system. Jack London's novel *The Iron Heel,* published in 1906, offered a vision of a socialist brotherhood of man. That same year Upton Sinclair published *The Jungle,* with a character who dreams of a socialist state. *The Jungle* also brought the shocking conditions in the Chicago meatpacking industry to the nation's attention. After it was published, the government passed laws to regulate the industry.

"Muckrakers" added to the mood of dissent, or disagreement with the system. These writers raked up the mud and muck—that is, the bad conduct and unfair practices—of corporations, government, and society in general. Then they exposed it to the world in newspaper and magazine articles or in books. Ida Tarbell, for example, wrote about the Standard Oil Company's business practices. Lincoln Steffens revealed political corruption in American cities.

(left)
Emma Goldman and
Alexander Berkman,
1918.

Sweatshops and Wobblies

BUSINESSES WERE LOOKING FOR WAYS TO produce more goods and make more money. One way was to break manufacturing down into a series of simple tasks. A worker would no longer make an entire piece of furniture, for example. Instead, he or she would simply repeat only one part of the work. So the worker would do the same task over and over again—maybe drilling a hole, or squirting glue. This way, companies could hire less skilled labor. Workers became interchangeable, almost like the machines they tended, stripped of individuality and humanity.

In New York City, many immigrants went to work in garment factories called sweatshops. In sweatshops, they worked for very low wages under unhealthy working conditions. They were paid based on how many pieces of clothing they sewed, not how many hours they worked. Many others did this piecework at home.

One of New York's five hundred sweatshops was the Triangle Shirtwaist Company. Women workers there went on strike in the winter of 1909. Twenty thousand other workers joined them. One striker, Pauline Newman, later recalled the scene. "Thousands upon thousands left the factories from every side," she wrote. "It was November, the cold winter was just around the corner, we had no fur coats to keep warm, and yet there was the spirit that led us on and on. . . ."

The strike lasted for months, against police, scabs, and arrests. Yet although the workers won some of their demands, conditions in the factories did not change much. In March 1911 a fire broke out in the Triangle building. The fire raged too high in the building for the fire department's ladders to reach it. With workroom doors illegally locked by the employers, the workers, mostly young women, were trapped. Some fled the flames by throwing themselves out windows. Others burned. When it was over, 146 had died. A hundred thousand New Yorkers marched in their memorial parade.

The union movement was growing, but the biggest union, the American Federation of Labor (AFL), did not represent all workers. Its members were almost all white, male, skilled laborers. Blacks were kept out of the AFL. Women made up a fifth of the workforce in 1910, but only one in a hundred women workers was in a union. In addition, AFL officials had begun to seem no better than corporate bosses. They were protected by "goon" squads who beat up union members who criticized them.

Working people who wanted radical change needed a new kind of union. At a 1905 meeting of anarchists, socialists, and unionists in Chicago, that union was born. It was called the Industrial Workers of the World (IWW), and its goal was to organize all workers in any industry into "One Big Union," undivided by sex, race, or skills.

The IWW came to be called the Wobblies, though it's not clear why. The Wobblies were brave, and they were willing to meet force with force. When they struck against the U.S. Steel Company in Pennsylvania in 1909, state troopers came to control the strike. The IWW vowed to kill a trooper for every striker who was killed. Three troopers and four strikers died in one gun battle, but the strikers stayed out until they won.

The IWW was inspired by a new idea that was developing in Spain, Italy, and France. This was anarcho-syndicalism, the belief that workers could take power in a country, not by seizing control of the government in an armed rebellion, but by bringing the economic system to a halt. The way to stop the economic system was by a general strike, one in which all workers in all the trades and industries would join, united by a common purpose.

In the ten exciting years after its birth, the IWW became a threat to the capitalist class in the United States. The union never had more than five or ten thousand members at a time, but their ability to organize strikes and protests made a big impact on the country. IWW organizers traveled everywhere—many of them were unemployed, or moved around as migrant workers. They sang, spoke, and spread their message and their spirit.

The IWW organizers suffered beatings, imprisonment, and even murder. A criminal case involving organizer Joe Hill gained world-wide attention. Hill was a songwriter whose funny, biting, and inspiring songs made him a legend. For example, "The Preacher and the Slave" had a favorite IWW target—the church, which often seemed to ignore the very real sufferings of the poor and working classes:

Long-haired preachers come out every night,
Try to tell you what's wrong and what's right;

Family members arrive at the New York City morgue to identify the bodies of victims of the Triangle Shirtwaist Company Fire, 1911.

But when asked how 'bout something to eat

They will answer with voices so sweet:

—You will eat, bye and bye,

—In that glorious land above the sky;

—Work and pray, live on hay,

—You'll get pie in the sky when you die.

In 1915 Hill was accused of killing a grocer in Salt Lake City, Utah, during a robbery. There was no direct evidence that he had committed the murder, but there were enough pieces of evidence for a jury to find him guilty. Ten thousand people wrote letters to the governor of Utah, protesting the verdict, but Joe Hill was executed by a firing squad. Before he died he wrote to Bill Haywood, another IWW leader, "Don't waste any time in mourning. Organize."

Socialism, Sex, and Race

LABOR STRUGGLES WERE ON THE RISE. IN the 1890s there had been about a thousand strikes a year. By 1904 there were four thousand.

Seeing the law and the military take the side of the rich again and again, hundreds of thousands of American began to think about socialism.

Socialism had gotten its start in the United States in cities in the small circles of Jewish and German immigrants. In time, though, it spread and became thoroughly American. As many as a million people across the country read socialist newspapers.

The Socialist political party formed in 1901. Eugene Debs, who had become a socialist after being jailed during a strike, became its spokesman. To Debs, the labor union meant much more than strikes and wage increases. Its goal was "to overthrow the capitalist system of private ownership of the tools of labor . . . and achieve the freedom of the whole working class and, in fact of all mankind."

Debs ran for president five times as the Socialist candidate. At one time his party had a hundred thousand members. The strongest state Socialist organization was in Oklahoma, where more than a hundred Socialists were elected to office.

Some of the feminists active in the women's rights movement in the early twentieth century were also socialists. They debated challenging questions: If the economic system changed, would women then be full equals in society? Was it better to work toward a revolutionary change in society or to fight for rights within the existing system? Many women were less concerned with social change than with suffrage, or the right to vote. At a friendly meeting with socialist leader Eugene Debs, feminist Susan B. Anthony said, "Give us suffrage, and we'll give you socialism." Debs replied, "Give us socialism and we'll give you suffrage."

Socialists like Helen Keller did not think suffrage was enough. Blind and deaf, Keller fought for change with her spirit and her pen. In 1911 she wrote, "Our democracy is but a name. We vote? What does that mean? . . . We choose between Tweedledum and Tweedledee."

Black women faced double oppression, held down because of their race as well as their sex. An African American nurse wrote to a newspaper in 1912:

> We poor colored women wage-earners in the South are
> fighting a terrible battle. . . . On the one hand, we are
> assailed by black men, who should be our natural
> protectors; and, whether in the cook kitchen, at the

washtub, over the sewing machine, behind the baby car-
riage, or at the ironing board, we are little more than
pack horses, beasts of burden, slaves!

The early part of the twentieth century was a
low point for African Americans, with lynchings
reported every week and murderous race riots in
places like Brownsville, Texas, and Atlanta,
Georgia. The government did nothing.

Blacks began to organize. In 1905 W. E. B. Du
Bois—a respected teacher and author who was
sympathetic to the socialists—called black leaders to a meeting in Canada, near Niagara Falls.
This was the start of the "Niagara Movement."
Five years later, a race riot in Springfield, Illinois,
led to the founding of the National Association
for the Advancement of Colored People
(NAACP). Whites dominated this new group. Du
Bois was the only black officer. The NAACP
focused on education and legal action to end
racism, but Du Bois represented the Niagara
Movement's strong spirit of activism.

The Progressive Movement
and the Colorado Coal Strike

BLACKS, FEMINISTS, LABOR UNIONS, AND
socialists saw clearly that they could not count on
the national government. And yet history books
give the label "Progressive Period" to the early
years of the twentieth century. True, it was a time
of reforms—but the reforms were made unwill-
ingly. They were not meant to bring about basic
changes in society, only to quiet the uprisings of
the people.

The period got the name "Progressive"
because new laws were passed. There were laws
for inspecting meat, regulating railroads, controlling the growth of monopolies, and keeping the
nation's food and medicines safe. Labor laws set
standards for wages and hours. Safety inspection
of workplaces and payment to employees
injured on the job were introduced. The U.S.
Constitution was changed so that U.S. senators
were elected directly by vote of the people, not by
state legislatures.

Ordinary people did benefit from these changes.
Basic conditions did not change, however, for the
vast majority of tenant farmers, factory workers,

slum dwellers, miners, farm laborers, and working men and women, black and white.

The government was still dedicated to protecting a system that benefited the upper classes. Theodore Roosevelt, for example, made a reputation as a "trust buster," a politician who opposed monopolies. But two men in the service of multimillionaire J. P. Morgan made private deals with Roosevelt to make sure that "trust-busting" wouldn't go too far. Roosevelt's advisers were industrialists and bankers, not unionists and workers.

The Progressive movement had some leaders who were honest reformers and others, like Roosevelt, who were only disguised as Progressives. In reality they were conservatives, opposed to change and concerned with preserving the balance of power and wealth. Both kinds of progressives saw their mission as fending off socialism. They felt that by improving conditions for the masses, they could prevent what one Progressive called "the menace of socialism."

The Socialist Party was on the rise. In 1910, Victor Berger became the first Socialist elected to the U.S. Congress. In 1911 there were seventy-three Socialist mayors and twelve hundred Socialists in other city and town offices. Newspapers talked about "The Rising Tide of Socialism."

The Progressives' goal was to save capitalism by repairing its worst problems. In this way, they thought, they could end the growing class war that pitted workers against the economic and political elites. But a strike of Colorado coal miners that began in September 1913 turned into one of the most bitter and violent battles in that war.

After a union organizer was murdered, eleven thousand miners went on strike. The Rockefeller family, which owned the mine, sent detectives with machine guns to raid the strikers' camps. The strikers fought to keep out strikebreakers and to keep the mines from opening. When the governor called on National Guard troops to destroy the strike, the Rockefellers paid the National Guards' wages.

Violent battles, betrayals, and massacres followed. In April 1914, the bodies of thirteen children and women were found in a pit, killed by a fire set by the National Guardsmen. The news spread across the country. Strikes, demonstrations, and protests broke out everywhere. President Woodrow Wilson finally sent in federal troops to crush the strike. Sixty-six men, women, and children had died. No soldier or mine guard was charged with a crime.

Colorado's ferocious class conflict was felt all over the land. Whatever reforms had been passed, whatever new laws were on the books, the threat of class rebellion remained—and unemployment and hard times were growing.

Could patriotism and the military spirit cover up class struggle? The nation was about to find out. In four months World War I would begin in Europe.

CHAPTER TWO

WORLD WAR I

THE NATIONS OF EUROPE WENT TO WAR IN
the late summer of 1914. The conflict that we now
call World War I would drag on for four years. Ten
million people would die on its battlefields.
Twenty million more would die of hunger and disease related to the war. And no one has ever been
able to show that the war brought any gain for
humanity that would be worth a single life.

At the time, socialists called it an "imperialist
war"—a war fought in the service of empire building, by nations that wanted to increase their power
by controlling territory or resources. The advanced
capitalist nations of Europe fought over bound-
aries, such as the region of Alsace-Lorraine,
claimed by both France and Germany. They fought
over colonies in Africa. And they fought over

(left, detail)
Eugene V. Debs
at a Labor Convention,
1910s.

"spheres of influence," areas in Eastern Europe and the Middle East that were not claimed openly as colonies but still came under the "protection" and control of some European nation.

Blood and Money

MANY NATIONS JOINED THE WAR ON ONE SIDE or the other, but the main enemies were Germany on one side and the Allies, France and Great Britain, on the other. The killing started very fast, and on a very large scale. In one early battle in France, each side had half a million casualties. Almost the entire British army from before the war was wiped out in the first three months of fighting.

The battle lines were drawn across France. For three years they barely moved. Men spent months in filthy, disease-ridden trenches. Each side would push forward, then be pushed back, then push forward again for a few yards or a few miles, while the corpses piled up. In 1916 the Germans tried to break through the lines at a place called Verdun.

The British and French counterattacked and lost six hundred thousand men.

The people of France and Britain were not told the full numbers of dead and wounded. When a German attack on the Somme River caused three hundred thousand British casualties in the last year of the war, London newspapers told readers, "Be cheerful. . . . Write encouragingly to friends at the front."

The same thing was true in Germany—the true horror of the war was kept from the people. On days when men were being blown apart in the thousands by machine guns and artillery shells, the official war reports said, "All Quiet on the Western Front." German writer Erich Maria Remarque later used that phrase as the title of his great novel about the war.

Into this pit of death and deception came the United States in 1917.

Earlier, President Woodrow Wilson had promised that the United States would keep out of the war. But the question of shipping in the North Atlantic Ocean drew the United States into the fight.

In 1915 a German submarine had torpedoed and sunk a British liner, the *Lusitania,* on its way from North America to Britain. Nearly 1,200 people,

including 124 Americans, died. The United States claimed that the *Lusitania* was carrying civilian passengers and innocent cargo, and that the German attack was a monstrous atrocity. In truth, the *Lusitania* was heavily armed. She carried thousands of cases of ammunition for the British. False cargo records hid this fact, and the British and American governments lied about the cargo.

Then, in April 1917, the Germans warned that their submarines would sink any ships that were carrying supplies to their enemies. This included the United States, which had been shipping huge amounts of war materials to Germany's enemies.

The war in Europe had been good for American business. A serious economic decline had hit the country in 1914, but things turned around when Americans began manufacturing war materials to sell to the Allies—mainly to Britain. By the time the Germans issued their warning about shipping, the United States had sold 2 billion dollars' worth of goods to the Allies. American prosperity was now tied to England's war. President Wilson said that he must stand by the right of Americans to travel on merchant ships in the war zone, and Congress declared war on Germany.

(left)
Eugene V. Debs
at a Labor Convention,
1910s.

Wilson called it a war "to end all wars" and "to make the world safe for democracy." These rousing words did not inspire Americans to enlist in the armed forces. A million men were needed, but in the first six weeks, only 73,000 volunteered. Congress authorized a draft to compel men into service. It also set up a Committee on Public Information. That committee's job was to convince Americans that the war was right.

The Radical Response

THE GOVERNMENT WANTED TO DISCOURAGE dissent and criticism of the war. It passed a law called the Espionage Act. The title makes it seem like a law against spying. But one part of the law called for up to twenty years in prison for anyone who refused to serve in the armed forces or even tried to convince others not to enlist. The act was used to imprison Americans who spoke or wrote against the war.

About nine hundred people went to prison under the Espionage Act. One of them was a Philadelphia socialist named Charles Schenck. Two months after the act became law, Schenck was sentenced to jail for printing and distributing fifteen thousand leaflets against the draft and the war. He appealed the verdict, claiming that the act violated his First Amendment rights to freedom of speech and freedom of the press. The case went to the Supreme Court.

All nine justices agreed. The Court decided against Schenck. Justice Oliver Wendell Holmes said that even the strict protection of free speech "would not protect a man in falsely shouting fire in a theatre and causing panic." This was a clever comparison. Few people would think that some- one should be allowed to get away with shouting "Fire!" in a crowded theater and causing a dan- gerous panic. But did that example fit criticism of the war?

Socialist Eugene Debs was also involved in a case before the Supreme Court. After visiting three socialists who were in prison for opposing the draft, he made a fiery antiwar speech in the street:

> They tell us that we live in a great free republic; that our
> institutions are democratic; that we are a free and self-gov-
> erning people. That is too much, even for a joke. . . . Wars
> throughout history have been waged for conquest and

plunder. . . . And that is war in a nutshell. The master class
has always declared the wars; the subject class has always
fought the battles. . . .

Debs was arrested for violating the Espionage
Act. At his trial he declared, "I have been accused
of obstructing the war. I admit it. Gentlemen, I
abhor war." The judge, in turn, spoke harshly
about "those who would strike the sword from the
hand of his nation while she is engaged in defend-
ing herself against a foreign and brutal power." He
sentenced Debs to ten years in prison. (Several
years later, after the war was over, President
Warren Harding released Debs from prison.)

The press worked with the government to create an atmosphere of fear for anyone who dared to
criticize the war. One publication asked its readers
to turn in any published material they saw that
seemed seditious, or disloyal, to the country. Men
joined the American Vigilante Patrol to "put an
end to seditious street oratory"—basically, to prevent antiwar speechmaking. The U.S. Post Office
took away the mailing privileges of newspapers
and magazines that published antiwar articles.
The Committee on Public Information tried to
turn people into spies and informers against each

other. It urged citizens to "report the man who spreads pessimistic stories. Report him to the Department of Justice."

The Department of Justice sponsored the American Protective League in six hundred towns. Its members were bankers and leading business-men. The League seized other people's mail, broke into their homes and offices, and claimed to find 3 million cases of "disloyalty." In 1918 the attorney general of the United States declared, "It is safe to say that never in its history has this country been so thoroughly policed."

Why these huge efforts? Because Americans were refusing to fight in the war. Senator Thomas Hardwick of Georgia described "general and widespread opposition on the part of many thousands . . . to the enactment of the draft law." Before the war was over, more than a third of a million men were classified as draft evaders—people who refused to be drafted, or used trick-ery or self-mutilation to avoid the draft.

The Socialist Party had been against entering the war from the start. The day after Congress declared war, the Socialists held an emergency meeting and called the declaration "a crime

WE MOURN
THE LOSS
OF OUR
COMRADES

FRANCISFERRER ASSOCIATION
OF BROWNSVILLE.

16877

Elizabeth Gurley Flynn
addressing crowd, 1914.

against the people of the United States." Some
well-known Socialists, including writers
Upton Sinclair and Jack London, supported
the war after the United States entered it.
Most Socialists, though, continued to oppose
the war. Some paid a heavy price for expressing
their opinions.

In Oklahoma, the Industrial Workers of the
World (IWW) planned a march on Washington
for people from across the country who objected
to the draft. Before the march, union members
were arrested. Four hunded and fifty people
accused of rebellion were put in the state peni-
tentiary. Across the country in Boston, eight
thousand Socialists and unionists at an antiwar
march were attacked by soldiers and sailors, acting on their officers' orders.

Just before the United States declared war, the
IWW newspaper had said, "Capitalists of America,
we will fight against you, not for you!" Now the war
gave the government its chance to destroy the radical union. In September 1917, Department of
Justice agents raided forty-eight IWW meeting halls
across the country, seizing letters and literature.

The following April, 101 leaders of the union

went on trial for opposing the draft and encouraging soldiers to desert. One of them told the court:

> You ask me why the IWW is not patriotic to the United States. If you were a bum without a blanket; if you had left your wife and kids when you went west for a job, and had never located them since; if your job had never kept you long enough in a place to qualify you to vote; if every person who represented law and order and the nation beat you up . . . how in hell do you expect a man to be patriotic? This war is a business man's war. . . .

All of the IWW prisoners were found guilty. Bill Haywood and other key leaders were sentenced to twenty years in prison; the rest received shorter sentences. Haywood fled to Russia, where a socialist revolution was taking place. The IWW in the United States was shattered.

After the Fighting

THE WAR ENDED IN NOVEMBER 1918. Fifty thousand American soldiers had died. But when the war was over, the Establishment—the

political and capitalist elites that ran the nation—
still feared socialism. The conflict between
Democrats and Republicans was less important
than the threat of radical change.

The government had a new tool to fight that
threat. Near the end of the war, Congress had
passed a law that let the government deport any
alien who opposed organized government or who
approved of the destruction of property. (An alien
was an immigrant who was not a U.S. citizen.
Deporting meant removing from the country.) In
1919 and 1920 the government rounded up more
than four thousand aliens, including anarchist
Emma Goldman. Eventually, they were deported
to their birth countries.

An anarchist named Andrea Salsedo was held
for two months in FBI offices in New York City.
He wasn't allowed to contact family, friends, or
lawyers. Then his crushed body was found on the
pavement. The FBI said he had committed suicide
by jumping from a window.

Two Boston anarchists, friends of Salsedo,
learned of his death and began carrying guns. They
were arrested and charged with a holdup and murder that had happened two weeks earlier. Their

names were Nicola Sacco and Bartolomeo Vanzetti.

Sacco and Vanzetti were found guilty. They spent seven years in jail while their cases were appealed to higher courts. All over the world, people became involved in the case. Many believed that Sacco and Vanzetti had been found guilty just because they were anarchists and foreigners—the trial record and other circumstances make it look as though this was true. In August 1927 the two men were executed.

The Establishment had tried to silence the voices of dissent. Reforms had been made. War had been used to promote patriotism and crush criticism. The courts and jails had made it clear that certain ideas, certain kinds of resistance, were not permitted. But still, even from the prison cells, the message was going out: in the United States, a society that was supposed to be without classes, the class war was going on.

CHAPTER THREE

HARD TIMES

IT WAS FEBRUARY 1919. THE WAR HAD
ended in Europe just a few months before. The
world was in the grip of an influenza epidemic
that would claim half a million American lives and
millions more worldwide. In the United States,
the leaders of the Industrial Workers of the World
were in jail—but their dream was about to become
a reality in Seattle, Washington.

Strikes by a single union or a single kind of worker
could get results. But the IWW felt that a general
strike, with all kinds of workers walking off their jobs
together, would make a stronger statement. In
Seattle, after shipyard workers went on strike for
higher wages, more than a hundred other unions
voted to strike as well. A walkout of a hundred thousand working people brought the city to a halt.

(left, detail)
A caravan of strike
pickets patrol
a road south
of Tulare, 1933.

The strikers kept vital services going. Fire fighters stayed on the job, and milk stations were set up in neighborhoods to deliver milk to families. The strike lasted for five days and was peaceful. In fact, during those five days, the city had less crime than usual. But after the strike, the authorities raided Socialist Party headquarters. Thirty-nine members of the IWW went to jail as "ring-leaders of anarchy."

Why did the government react this way to the strike? Maybe the answer lies in a statement by Seattle's mayor:

> The general strike, as practiced in Seattle, is of itself the weapon of revolution, all the more dangerous because quiet. To succeed, it must suspend everything; stop the entire life stream of a community. . . . That is to say, it puts the government out of operation.

The general strike made the authorities feel powerless. It seemed to threaten the whole economic and political system of society.

Seattle's general strike was just one of many large strikes across the United States in 1919. These labor actions were part of a wave of rebellions around the world. From the Communist revolution against royal rule in Russia to a strike by railway workers in England, ordinary people were rising up, making their voices heard, and bringing about change. A writer for *The Nation* magazine said, "The common man . . . losing faith in the old leadership, has experienced a new . . . self-confidence. . . ."

The Truth about the Twenties

When the 1920s started, the wave of rebellion had died down in the United States. The IWW was destroyed. The Socialist Party was falling apart. Strikes were beaten down by force. The economy was doing just well enough for just enough people to prevent mass rebellion.

The 1920s are sometimes called the Roaring Twenties, or the Jazz Age—a time of prosperity and fun. There was some truth to that picture. Unemployment was down, and the general level of workers' wages went up. People could buy new gadgets such as automobiles, radios, and refrigerators. Millions of people were not doing badly.

But most of the wealth was in the hands of a few people at the top of society's pyramid. At the

bottom of the pyramid were the black and white tenant farmers living in poverty in the country-side, and the immigrant families in the cities who could not find work, or could not earn enough for basic needs. In New York City alone, 2 million people lived in tenement buildings that were known to be unsafe because of fire danger.

Fourteen million immigrants had come to the United States between 1900 and 1920. In 1924, Congress passed an immigration law that put an end to this flood. The new law favored the immi-gration of white people from English and German backgrounds. Immigration of Southern Europeans, Slavs, and Jews was severely limited, and only a hundred people a year could come from China or any African country.

Racial hatred and violence were everywhere. The Ku Klux Klan came back in the 1920s, and it spread into the North. By 1924 it had 4.5 mil-lion members.

After a long struggle, women had finally won the right to vote in national elections in 1920. Yet voting was still an upper-class and middle-class activity, and the new women voters favored the same old political parties as other voters.

(left)
A caravan of strike pickets patrol a road south of Tulare, 1933.

Labor unrest may have calmed for a time, but it had not faded away. With the Socialist Party weakened, a Communist Party formed in the United States. Communists were involved in many labor struggles, including huge textile strikes in Tennessee and the Carolinas in early 1929.

The Great Depression

DURING THE 1920S, THE AMERICAN ECONOMY seemed healthy—even booming. Prices for stocks, which are shares of ownership in corporations, rose higher than ever. Many people thought that the value of stocks would just keep going up. They invested their money by buying stocks, and they borrowed money from banks to buy still more stocks. The banks invested in stocks, too, using the money that customers had deposited.

In 1929 the boom ended with a crash. When the value of stocks started to drop, people started selling their stocks in a panic. This made the value drop even faster. Banks could not collect the loans that people had taken to buy stocks, and people could not withdraw their money from banks that had invested it and lost it. Both the stock market and the banking system spiraled swiftly downward, triggering a severe crisis in the economy. The United States had entered the Great Depression.

The economy was stunned, barely moving. More than five thousand banks closed. Thousands of businesses closed, too. Businesses that managed to stay open laid off some workers and cut the wages of other workers, again and again. By 1933 perhaps as many as 15 million people were out of work. A quarter to a third of the nation's workforce could not find jobs.

There were millions of tons of food in the country, but it was not profitable to ship it or sell it, so people went hungry. Warehouses were full of clothing and other products, but people couldn't afford to buy them. Houses stayed empty because no one had the money to buy or rent them. People who failed to pay rent were kicked out of their homes. They lived in "Hoovervilles," communities of shacks built on garbage dumps. The name comes from President Herbert Hoover, who had said just before the crash, "We in America today

RARIG'S KID
DOESN'T STARVE
WHY SHOULD WE?
WHY CAN'T
GIVE MY DA
A JOB?

are nearer to the final triumph over poverty than ever before in the history of any land."

One of the few politicians who had spoken out for the poor during the 1920s was Fiorello La Guardia, a congressman from a district of poor immigrants in East Harlem. After the Depression started, he received a letter from a tenement dweller there:

> You know my condition is bad. I used to get pension from the government and they stopped it. It is now nearly seven months I am out of work. I hope you will try to do something for me. . . . I have four children who are in need of clothes and food. . . . My daughter who is eight is very ill and not recovering. My rent is due two months and I am afraid of being put out.

Hard times made people desperate. In *The Grapes of Wrath*, a novel about the misery of Oklahoma farmers forced off their land, author John Steinbeck called the new homeless people "dangerous." A spirit of rebellion was growing in the land.

In Detroit, five hundred men rioted when they were turned out of public housing because they couldn't afford to pay for it. In Chicago, five hundred schoolchildren, "most with haggard faces and in tattered clothes," marched through down-

(left) Children carry picket signs at a demonstration for the Workers Alliance during the Great Depression, 1937.

town to demand food from the school system. In New York City, several hundred jobless people surrounded a restaurant, demanding to be fed without charge. In Seattle, an army of the unemployed seized a public building and held it for two days.

Men who had fought in the First World War now found themselves out of work and out of money. Some held certificates from the government that were to be paid off in the future—but they needed the money now. And so war veterans began to move toward Washington, D.C., from all over the country. They came in broken-down old autos, or by stealing rides on trains, or by hitchhiking.

More than twenty thousand came. They camped across from the Capitol, in shelters made of old boxes and newspapers. President Hoover ordered the army to get rid of them. General Douglas A. MacArthur, with the help of officers such as Dwight D. Eisenhower and George S. Patton, used tanks, tear gas, and fires to break up the camp. When it was over, two veterans had been shot to death, a boy was partially blinded, two police had fractured skulls, and a thousand veterans were injured by gas.

Struggling to Survive

IN THE ELECTION OF 1932, HOOVER LOST TO
the Democratic candidate, Franklin D. Roosevelt,
who launched a series of reform laws that came to
be called the New Deal. These reforms went far
beyond earlier changes. They attempted to reor-
ganize capitalism.

The first major law was the National Recovery
Act (NRA). It took control of the economy by making government, management, and labor agree on
such things as prices, wages, and competition.
From the start, the NRA was controlled by big
business, but it did give some benefits to working
people. Two years later, though, the Supreme
Court declared the NRA unconstitutional because
it gave too much power to the president.

Other reforms continued. One was the
Tennessee Valley Authority, (TVA) which built a
government-owned system of dams and power
plants. The TVA provided jobs and lower electricity rates. Its critics called it "socialistic," and they
were right in some ways.

The New Deal had two goals. The first was to
overcome the Depression and make the economy
more stable. The second was to give enough help

HARD TIMES

to the lower classes to keep rebellion from turning into a real revolution.

The rebellion was real when Roosevelt took office. All across the country, people were not waiting for the government to help them. They were helping themselves.

In Detroit and Chicago, when police removed the furniture of people who had been evicted from their apartments for not paying rent, crowds gathered on the sidewalk to carry the furniture back inside. In Seattle, fishermen, fruit pickers, and woodchoppers traded with each other for supplies they needed. Often labor unions helped make these self-help arrangements.

Self-help sprouted in the coal mines of Pennsylvania. Teams of unemployed miners dug small mines on company property, hauled the coal to the cities, and sold it for less than the companies charged. When the authorities tried to halt the trade in "bootleg" coal, local juries would not convict the miners, and local jailors would not imprison them. These were simple actions, but they had revolutionary possibilities. Working people were discovering a powerful truth: that they could meet their own needs. Soon, though, a wave of large-scale labor outbursts caused the government to get involved in the labor movement.

It began with strikes by West Coast longshoremen—workers who loaded and unloaded cargo ships. They struck, tying up two thousand miles of coastline. A general strike in San Francisco followed, then another in Minneapolis, and then the biggest strike of all: 325,000 textile workers in the South.

New unions formed among workers who had never been organized. Black farmers were hit very hard by the Depression. Some were attracted to the strangers who started showing up, suggesting that they unionize. Hosea Hudson, a black man from rural Georgia who had worked the land from the age of ten, joined the Communist Party and helped organize unemployed blacks in Birmingham, Alabama. Later he recalled those years of activism:

> Block committees would meet every week, had a regular meeting. We talked about the welfare question, what was happening, we read the *Daily Worker* and the *Southern Worker* to see what was going on about unemployed relief. . . . We kept it up, we was on top, so people always wanted to come cause we had something different to tell them each time.

In many strikes, the decision to act came from the rank and file—the ordinary members—not from the union leaders. Rubber workers in Akron, Ohio, came up with a new kind of strike called a sit-down. Instead of leaving the plant and marching outside, they remained inside and did not work.

The longest sit-down strike took place among autoworkers in Michigan. Starting in December 1936 for forty days there was a community of two thousand strikers. "It was like war," one of them said. "The guys with me became my buddies." Committees organized recreation, classes, postal service, and sanitation. A restaurant owner across the street prepared three meals a day. Armed workers circled the plant outside, fighting off a police attack. Finally the strikers and management agreed to a six-month contract, and the strike ended.

To bring a halt to this type of labor unrest, the government set up the National Labor Relations Board (NLRB). The NLRB would recognize the legal status of unions, listen to their complaints, and settle some of their issues. At the same time, the unions themselves were trying to become more influential, even respectable. Leaders of the major associations, the American Federation of Labor

(AFL) and the Congress of Industrial Organizations
(CIO), wanted to keep strikes to a minimum. They
began channeling workers' rebellious energy into
things like contract talks and meetings.

Some historians of the labor movement claim
that workers won most during the early years of
rank-and-file uprisings, before unions were recog-
nized and well organized. While the AFL and the
CIO each had more than 6 million members by
1945, their power was less than it had been before.
Gains from the use of strikes kept getting whittled
down. The NLRB leaned more toward the side of
management than toward labor, the Supreme
Court ruled that sit-down strikes were illegal, and
state governments passed laws that made striking
and picketing more difficult.

By the late 1930s, the worst of the Depression
had passed for some people. New laws passed in
1938 limited the work week to forty hours and outlawed child labor. The Social Security Act gave
retirement benefits and unemployment insurance
(but not to everyone—farmers, for example, were
left out). There was a new minimum wage, and
the government built some housing projects.
These measures didn't help everyone who needed

help, but they made people feel that something was being done.

Black people gained little from the New Deal. Many worked as tenant farmers, farm laborers, domestic workers, and migrants. They did not qualify for the minimum wage or unemployment insurance. Blacks suffered job discrimination—they were the last to be hired and the first to be fired. Lynchings continued, and so did less violent forms of racial prejudice.

In the mid-1930s a young black poet named Langston Hughes gave voice to frustration and hope in a poem called "Let America Be America Again":

> . . . I am the poor white, fooled and pushed apart,
>
> I am the Negro bearing slavery's scars.
>
> I am the red man driven from the land,
>
> I am the immigrant clutching the hope I seek—
>
> And finding only the same old stupid plan.
>
> Of dog eat dog, of mighty crush the weak. . . .
>
> O, let America be America again—
>
> The land that never has been yet—

The New Deal had brought an exciting flowering of the arts, such as had never happened before in American history. Federal money was used to pay thousands of writers, artists, musicians, and photographers for creative projects. Working-class audiences saw plays and heard symphonies for the first time. But by 1939, the arts programs ended. The country was more stable, and the New Deal was over.

Capitalism had not changed. The rich still controlled the nation's wealth, as well as its laws, courts, police, newspapers, churches, and colleges. Enough help had been given to make Roosevelt a hero to millions, but the system that had brought the Great Depression remained in place.

Elsewhere in the world, war was brewing. German leader Adolf Hitler was on the march in Europe. Across the Pacific, Japan was invading China. For the United States, war was not far off.

CHAPTER FOUR

WORLD WAR II
AND THE COLD WAR

WORLD WAR I WAS ONLY ABOUT TWENTY YEARS
in the past when another huge war began in
Europe. Some call it the most popular war the
United States ever fought. Eighteen million
Americans served in the armed forces, and 25 million gave money from their paychecks to support
the war.

It was a war against evil—the evil of Germany's
Nazi Party, led by Adolf Hitler. After coming to
power in Germany, the Nazis began attacking Jews
and members of other minorities. Hitler's
Germany became a war machine, determined to
conquer other countries. For the United States to
step forward to defend those helpless people and
countries matched the image of the nation in
American schoolbooks, but is that what really

happened? Are there other ways to look at World War II, questions that did not get asked in the patriotic excitement of the time?

America at War

THE WAR STARTED IN 1939 AFTER GERMANY attacked Poland. Germany had already taken over Austria and Czechoslovakia. Later the Germans would invade and occupy France. Italy had already invaded the African nation of Ethiopia. Together with some smaller powers, Germany and Italy formed one side in the conflict. They were known as the Axis. Against them stood the Allies. Britain was one of the main Allied powers. Another was Russia, which now had a Communist government and had been renamed the Soviet Union.

The other side of the world was at war, too. Japan had attacked China and was moving toward Southeast Asia, which had rich resources of tin, rubber, and oil.

What did the United States do while this was happening? Hitler's attacks on the Jews did not bring the United States into the war. Neither did Germany's invasions of other countries, although President Franklin D. Roosevelt sent American aid to Britain. Neither did Japan's attack on China.

The United States entered the war after the Japanese attacked an American naval base at Pearl Harbor, Hawaii, on December 7, 1941. This strike at a link in the American Pacific empire was the reason the United States joined the fight, in Europe as well as Asia.

Once the United States had joined with England and Russia in the war, what were its goals? Was America fighting for humanitarian reasons or for power and profit? Was it fighting to end the control of some nations by others—or to make sure that the controlling nations were friends of the United States?

Noble statements about the government's goals didn't always match the things that were said privately. In August of 1941, Roosevelt and the British prime minister, Winston Churchill, announced their goals for the world after the war. They said that they respected "the right of all peoples to choose the form of government under which they will live." But two weeks earlier, a top U.S. government official had quietly promised the French government that France would regain its empire of overseas territories after the war.

Italy had bombed cities when it invaded Ethiopia. German planes had dropped bombs on cities in the Netherlands and England. These were not attacks on military targets. They were attacks on the civilian population. Roosevelt had called them "inhuman barbarism that has profoundly shocked the conscience of humanity."

But the German bombings were very small compared with British and American bombings of German cities. Raids of a thousand planes or more targeted cities. They did not even pretend to be seeking only military targets. The climax of the Allied terror bombing was an attack on the German city Dresden. More than a hundred thousand people died in a firestorm started by the bombs.

During the war, newspaper headlines were full of battles and troop movements. Behind the headlines, American diplomats and businessmen worked hard to make sure that when the war ended American economic power would be second to none in the world. At the time, the poet Archibald MacLeish was an assistant secretary of state. He wrote:

> As things are now going, the peace we will make, the peace we seem to be making, will be a peace of oil, a peace of gold, a peace of shipping, a peace, in brief . . . without moral purpose or human interest. . . .

Many people thought that the reason for the war against the Axis was to end the terrible situation of Jews in German-occupied Europe. But that wasn't a chief concern of Roosevelt. While Jews were being put in concentration camps, and Germany was getting ready to begin exterminating 6 million Jews (and millions of other minorities and dissidents) in what has come to be called the Holocaust, Roosevelt failed to take steps to save some of those doomed lives. He left it to the U.S. State Department, which did nothing.

Hitler claimed that the white German race—he called it Aryan or Nordic—was superior to others. Was the war being fought to show that his ideas of racial superiority were wrong? American blacks might not have thought so. The nation's armed forces were segregated by race. Even the blood

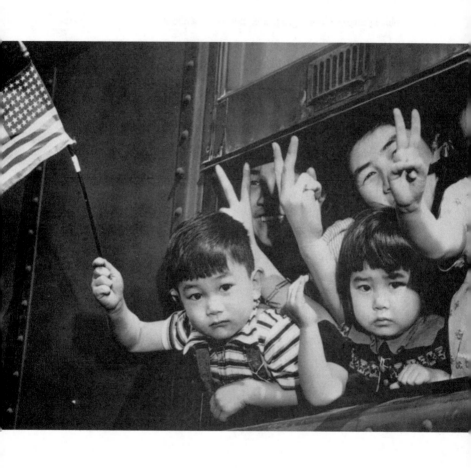

banks that saved thousands of lives kept blood from white people apart from blood donated by black people. A black doctor named Charles Drew had invented the blood-bank system, but when he tried to end blood segregation, he was fired.

Blacks in the United States knew the reality of racial prejudice, and sometimes racial violence, in everyday life. In 1943 an African American newspaper printed a poem about the thoughts of a black man drafted into the army:

> Dear Lord, today
>
> I go to war:
>
> To fight, to die,
>
> Tell me what for?
>
> Dear Lord, I'll fight,
>
> I do not fear,
>
> Germans or Japs;
>
> My fears are here.
>
> America!

In the way it treated Japanese Americans during the war, the United States came close to the brutal, racist oppression that it was supposed to be fighting against. After the attack on Pearl Harbor, anti-Japanese feeling was strong in the government. One congressman said, "I'm for catching every

(*left*)
Japanese American citizens on their way to an internment camp flash "victory" signs, 1942.

Japanese in America, Alaska and Hawaii now and putting them in concentration camps. . . . Let's get rid of them!"

In 1942 Roosevelt gave the army the power to arrest every Japanese American on the West Coast—eleven thousand men, women, and children. Three-fourths of them had been born in the United States and were U.S. citizens. The others, born in Japan, could not become U.S. citizens because American law made that impossible.

The Japanese were taken from their homes and carried to camps in remote regions of the interior. There they were kept in prison conditions. They remained in those camps for more than three years.

The war in Europe ended in May 1945 when a beaten Germany surrendered to the Allies. By August of that year, Japan also was in desperate shape and ready to surrender. But there was one problem. The Japanese emperor was a holy figure to many of his people, and Japan wanted to keep him in place after a surrender. If the United States had agreed, Japan would have stopped the war. But the United States refused, and the fighting continued. (After the war, the United States allowed the emperor to remain anyway.)

Japan did give up—after the United States dropped atomic bombs on the cities of Hiroshima and Nagasaki in August of 1945. The bombs killed as many as 150,000 people and left countless others to die slowly of radiation poisoning. It was the first use of these deadly new weapons in war.

Why would the United States not take the small step of allowing Japan to keep its emperor if that would have ended the war without the use of atomic weapons? Was it because too much money and work had gone into the atomic bomb not to use it? Or was it because the United States wanted to end the war before the Soviet Union could enter the fight against Japan, as it planned to do? If Japan surrendered to the Soviet Union, then the Russians, not the Americans, would control postwar Japan.

Whatever the real reasons for dropping atomic bombs on Japan, at least the war was over. Or was it?

The War at Home

THE WAR YEARS WERE A PATRIOTIC TIME IN
the United States. The country seemed totally dedicated to winning the war. There was no organized antiwar movement. Only one socialist group came out firmly against the war. It was the Socialist Workers Party. In 1943 eighteen of its members went to jail under a law that made it a crime to join any group that called for "the overthrow of government by force and violence."

Still, many people thought the war was wrong. About 350,000 of them avoided the draft. More than forty thousand flatly refused to fight.

The nation's two biggest groups of labor unions, the AFL and the CIO, had pledged not to go out on strike during the war. Yet there were more strikes during wartime than at any other time in American history. In 1944 alone, more than a million workers walked off their jobs in mines, steel mills, and manfuacturing plants. Many were angry that their wages stayed the same while the companies that made weapons and other war materials were earning huge profits.

By the end of the war, things seemed better to a lot of people. The war had brought big corporate

WORLD WAR II AND THE COLD WAR

(*left*)
Ethel and Julius Rosenberg leaving New York City Federal Court after arraignment, 1950.

profits, but it also had brought higher prices for farm crops, wage increases for some workers, and enough prosperity for enough people to keep them from becoming rebellious. It was an old lesson learned by governments—war solves the problem of controlling the citizens. The president of the General Electric Corporation suggested that business and the military should create "a permanent wartime economy."

That's just what happened. The public was tired of war, but its new president, Harry S. Truman, built a mood of crisis that came to be called the Cold War. In the Cold War, America's enemy was the Communist country that had been its ally in World War II, the Soviet Union.

New Wars

THE RIVALRY WITH THE SOVIET UNION WAS real. The former Russia was making an amazing comeback from the war. It was rebuilding its economy and regaining military strength. But the Truman administration presented the Soviet Union as something worse than a rival. The Soviet Union, and communism itself, were seen as immediate threats.

The U.S. government encouraged fear of communism. Any communism-related revolutionary movement in Europe or Asia was made to look as if the Soviets were taking over more of the world. When Communist-led revolutionaries gained control of the Chinese government in 1949, China became the world's most populous Communist nation—and added fuel to Americans' fear.

The growing fear of Soviet power and communism in general led to a big increase in U.S. military spending. It also led to new political partnerships between conservatives and liberals.

In politics, a conservative is someone who wants to preserve the existing order of society, government, and the economy. Conservatives tend to place a high value on security, stability, and established institutions. A liberal is someone who supports progress, often through change. If the changes are extreme, a liberal may be called a radical. Liberals tend to place a high value on individual rights, civil liberties, and direct participation in government. (The liberal position has come to be called the Left, while the conservative position is the Right.)

The United States wanted to unite conservatives and liberals, Republicans and Democrats, in support of the Cold War and the fight against communism. Events in the Asian nation of Korea helped President Truman get that support.

After World War II, Korea had been freed from Japanese control and divided into two countries. North Korea was a socialist dictatorship, part of the Soviet Union's sphere of influence. South Korea was a conservative dictatorship in the American sphere of influence. In 1950 North Korea invaded South Korea. The United Nations— which had been created during the war and was dominated by the United States—asked its member nations to help South Korea. Truman sent U.S. forces, and the United Nations army became the American army.

When American forces pushed all the way through North Korea to the Chinese border, China entered the fighting on the side of North Korea. In three years, the war killed as many as 2 million Koreans and reduced North and South Korea to ruins. Yet when the fighting ended in 1953, the boundary between the two Koreas was where it had been before.

If the Korean War changed little in Korea, it had an effect in the United States. It caused many liberals to join with conservatives in supporting the president, the war, and the military economy. This meant trouble for radical critics who stayed outside the circle of agreement.

The Left had become a force during the Depression and the war. The Communist Party probably never had more than about a hundred thousand members, but it had influence in the labor unions, in the arts, and among Americans who had seen the failure of capitalism in the 1930s. To make capitalism more secure, to build support for an American victory over Communist foes, the nation's established powers of government and business had to weaken the Left. They did so by attacking communism. The hunt for Reds, as Communists were called, soon filled American life.

In 1947 Truman launched a program to search out "disloyal persons" in the U.S. government. In the next five years, more than 6.5 million government employees were investigated. In their book

The Fifties, historians Douglas Miller and Marion Nowack described the results:

> Not a single case of espionage was uncovered, though about 500 persons were dismissed in dubious cases of "questionable loyalty." All of this was conducted with secret evidence, secret and often paid informers, and neither judge nor jury. . . . A conservative and fearful reaction coursed the country. Americans became convinced of the need for absolute security and the preservation of the established order.

World events built support for this anti-Communist crusade. Communist parties came to power in places like Czechoslovakia and China. Revolutionary movements flared up in Asia and Africa when colonial peoples demanded independence from European powers. These events were presented to the American public as signs of a worldwide Communist plot.

Senator Joseph McCarthy of Wisconsin began his own crusade to find Communist traitors in the country's State Department and the military. He found nothing and eventually became an embarrassment to the government. Other political leaders, however, had their own ideas for crushing dissent. Liberal senators Hubert Humphrey and Herbert Lehman suggested that suspected Communists and traitors could be held without trial in concentration camps. The camps were set up, ready for use.

The government also made lists of hundreds of organizations it considered suspicious. Anyone who joined these groups, or even seemed sympathetic to them, could be investigated. Leaders of the Communist Party were jailed.

In 1950 the government charged Julius and Ethel Rosenberg, known to be connected with the Communist Party, with giving atomic secrets to the Soviets. Although the evidence against the Rosenbergs was weak, they were executed as spies. Later investigations proved that the case was deeply flawed. But at the time, everything from movies and comic strips to history lessons and newspapers urged Americans to fight communism.

By 1960, the Establishment seemed to have succeeded in weakening the Left. The Communist-radical upsurge of the New Deal and the wartime years had been broken up. The Cold War kept the country in a permanent war economy. There were big pockets of poverty, but enough people were

WORLD WAR II AND THE COLD WAR

making enough money to keep things quiet.
Everything seemed under control. And then, in
the 1960s, rebellions exploded in every area of
American life.

70

CHAPTER FIVE

BLACK REVOLT
AND CIVIL RIGHTS

THE BLACK REVOLT OF THE 1950S AND 1960S surprised white America, but it shouldn't have. When people are oppressed, memory is the one thing that can't be taken away from them. For people with memories of oppression, revolt is always just an inch below the surface.

Blacks in the United States had the memory of slavery. Beyond that, they lived with the daily realities of lynching, insults, and segregation. As the twentieth century went on, they found new ways to resist.

Fighting Back

In the 1920s a black poet named Claude McKay
wrote these lines:

> If we must die, let it not be like hogs
>
> Hunted and penned in an inglorious spot. . . .
>
> Like men we'll face the murderous cowardly pack,
>
> Pressed to the wall, dying, but fighting back!

McKay's words were entered into the
Congressional Record as an example of the dangerous new ideas of young black men. It must have
seemed dangerous to the nation's leaders that
blacks spoke of fighting back.

Some blacks fought the system by joining the
Communist Party. The Communists had been
active in the South. They had helped defend the
"Scottsboro Boys," nine young black men falsely
accused of rape in Alabama. Among the well-
known African Americans connected to the
Communist Party were the scholar W. E. B.
DuBois and the actor and singer Paul Robeson.

During the 1930s the Communists organized
committees to seek help for the needy. An organizer named Angelo Herndon was arrested and
charged with promoting revolution. He recalled
his trial:

They questioned me in great detail. Did I believe that the bosses and government ought to pay insurance to unemployed workers? That Negroes should have complete equality with white people? Did I feel that the working-class could run the mills and mines and government? That it wasn't necessary to have bosses at all?

I told them I believed all of that—and more. . . .

Herndon spent five years in prison before the Supreme Court ruled that the law he had been arrested for breaking was unconstitutional. To the Establishment, men like Herndon were signs of a frightening new mood among blacks. That mood was militancy—a willingness to fight.

Toward Civil Rights

PRESIDENT HARRY TRUMAN KNEW THAT THE United States had to do something about race for two reasons. One reason was to calm the frustrated black people of the United States. The other reason had to do with America's image in the world.

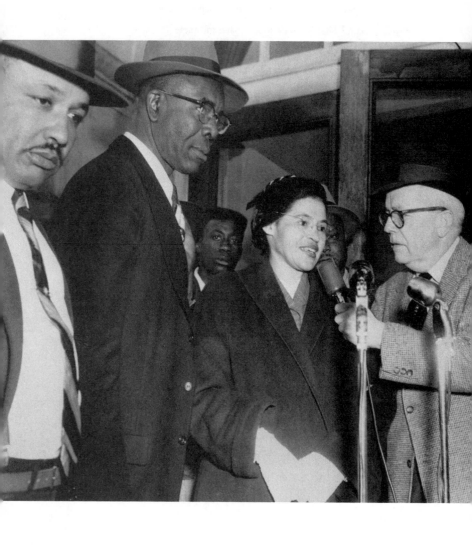

Nonwhite people around the world were accusing the United States of being a racist society. America's Cold War with the Soviet Union was on, and each side wanted to gain influence around the globe. But the poor civil rights record of the United States could hold it back in world politics.

Truman created a Committee on Civil Rights in 1946. The committee recommended laws against lynching and against racial discrimination in jobs and voting. Congress took no action. However, Truman did order the armed forces to desegregate, or end racial separation. It took ten years, but the military was finally integrated, with blacks and whites no longer separated.

The nation's public schools remained segregated until courageous southern blacks took on the Supreme Court in a series of lawsuits. In 1954, in a decision called *Brown v. Board of Education,* the Court ordered the nation's public schools to stop the "separate but equal" treatment of children separated by race. The Court's big decision sent a message around the world—the U.S. government had outlawed segregation. But change came slowly. Ten years later, more than three-fourths of the school districts in the South were still segregated.

(left)
Rosa Parks speaks with an interviewer as she arrives at court, 1956.

For blacks, progress wasn't fast enough. In the early 1960s black people rose in rebellion all over the South. By the late 1960s there were wild uprisings in a hundred northern cities, too. What triggered this angry revolt?

A forty-three-year-old black woman named Rosa Parks sat down one day in the "white" section of a city bus. She had long been active in the NAACP, which was determined to challenge segregated seating on Montgomery buses. She was arrested.

Montgomery's blacks called a mass meeting. They boycotted the city buses, refusing to ride. Instead, they walked or organized car pools. The city was losing a lot of income from bus fares. It arrested a hundred of the boycott leaders.

White segregationists turned to violence. They exploded bombs in four black churches. They fired a shotgun through the front door of the home of Dr. Martin Luther King Jr., a minister who helped lead the boycott. But the black people of Montgomery kept up the boycott, and in November 1956 the Supreme Court made segregation on local bus lines illegal.

Martin Luther King Preaches Nonviolence

AT A MEETING DURING THE BOYCOTT, MARTIN
Luther King showed the gift of speech making that
would soon inspire millions of people to work for
racial justice. He said:

> We have known humiliation, we have known abusive
> language, we have been plunged into the abyss of
> oppression. And we decided to raise up only with the
> weapon of protest. . . . We must use the weapon of love.
> We must have compassion and understanding for
> those who hate us.

King called on African Americans to practice
nonviolence—to seek justice without doing harm
to others. This message won him followers among
whites as well as blacks. Yet some blacks thought
that King's message was too simple. Some of
those who oppressed them, they believed, would
have to be bitterly fought.

Still, in the years after the Montgomery bus
boycott, southern blacks stressed nonviolence.
One nonviolent movement started in 1960, when
four first-year students at an African American
college in North Carolina decided to sit down at a
drugstore lunch counter where only whites ate.
The store wouldn't serve them, but they did not

Reverend Martin Luther King Jr. waves to participants in the Civil Rights Movement's March on Washington, 1963.

leave. They came back, joined by others, day after day, to sit at the counter.

Sit-ins spread to other southern cities. The sit-inners experienced violence. But they inspired more than fifty thousand people—mostly blacks, some whites—to join demonstrations in a hundred cities. By the end of 1960, lunch counters were open to blacks in many places.

Freedom Riders and the Mississippi Summer

FOR A LONG TIME, IT HAD BEEN ILLEGAL TO segregate people by race during long-distance travel. But the federal government had never enforced the law in the South, where blacks and whites were still kept apart on interstate buses. In the spring of 1961, a group of black and white pro-testors set out to change that.

These Freedom Riders got on a bus in Washington, D.C., bound for New Orleans. They never reached New Orleans. Riders were beaten in South Carolina. A bus was set on fire in Alabama.

Segregationists attacked the Riders with fists and iron bars. The southern police did nothing. Neither did the federal government, even though FBI agents watched the violence.

Young people who had taken part in the sit-ins formed the Student Nonviolent Coordinating Committee (SNCC). They organized another group of Freedom Riders, who were attacked by a mob of whites and later arrested. By this time the Freedom Riders were in the news all over the world.

Young black children joined demonstrations across the South. In Albany, Georgia, a small town where the atmosphere of slavery lingered, blacks held marches and mass meetings. After arresting protestors, the police chief took their names. One protestor was a boy about nine years old. "What's your name?" the police chief asked. The boy looked straight at him and answered, "Freedom, Freedom." A new generation was learning how to demand its rights.

The SNCC and other civil rights groups worked in Mississippi to register blacks for voting and to organize protests against racial injustice. They called on young people from other parts of the country to help, to come south for a "Mississippi

Summer." Facing increasing violence and danger, in June of 1964 they asked President Lyndon B. Johnson and Attorney General Robert Kennedy for federal protection. They got no answer.

Soon afterward, three civil rights workers, one black and two white, were arrested in Philadelphia, Mississippi. After being let out of jail late at night, they were beaten with chains and shot to death. Later the sheriff, deputy sheriff, and others went to jail for the murders.

Black Power

THE NATIONAL GOVERNMENT HAD REFUSED, again and again, to defend blacks against violence. Still, the uproar about civil rights, and the attention it drew around the world, made Congress pass some civil rights laws, including the Civil Rights Act of 1964. These laws promised much but were ignored or poorly enforced. Then, in 1965, a stronger Voting Rights Act made a difference in southern voting. In 1952, only 20 percent of blacks who could vote had registered to do so. But by 1968, 60 percent were registered—the same percentage as white voters.

The federal government was trying to control an explosive situation without making any basic changes. It wanted to channel black anger into traditional places, such as voting booths and quiet meetings with official support.

One meeting like that had taken place in 1963, when Martin Luther King led a huge march on Washington, D.C. The crowd thrilled to King's magnificent "I have a dream" speech, but the speech lacked the anger that many blacks felt. John Lewis was a young SNCC leader who had been arrested and beaten many times in the fight for racial equality. Lewis wanted the meeting to express some outrage, but its leaders wouldn't let him criticize the national government.

Two months later, a black militant named Malcolm X gave his view of the march on Washington:

> The Negroes were out there in the streets. They were talking about how they were going to march on Washington. . . .
>
> It was the grass roots out there in the street. It scared the

white man to death, scared the white power structure in
Washington, D.C. to death. . . .

This is what they did with the march on Washington.
They joined it . . . became part of it, took it over. . . . It
became a picnic, a circus. Nothing but a circus, with
clowns and all. . . . It was a takeover . . . they told the
Negroes what time to hit town, where to stop, what signs
to carry, what song to sing, what speech they could make,
and what speech they couldn't make, and then told them
to get out of town by sundown.

People were still exploding bombs in black
churches, killing children. The new "civil rights"
laws weren't changing the basic conditions of life
for black people.

Nonviolence had worked in the southern civil
rights movement, partly by turning the country's opinion against the segregationist South.
But by 1965, half of all African Americans lived
in the North. There were deep problems in the
ghettos, the poor black neighborhoods, of the
nation's cities.

In the summer of 1965, the ghetto of Watts, Los
Angeles, erupted with rioting in the streets and
with looting and firebombing of stores. Thirty-
four people were killed. Most of them were black.

More outbreaks took place the next year. In 1967, the biggest urban riots in American history broke out in black ghettos across the land. Eighty-three people died of gunfire, mostly in Newark, New Jersey, and Detroit, Michigan.

Martin Luther King was still respected, but new heroes were replacing him. "Black Power" was their slogan. They distrusted "progress" that was given a little at a time by whites. They rejected the idea that whites knew what was best for blacks.

Malcolm X was Black Power's chief spokesman. He was assassinated in 1965, while giving a speech. After his death, millions read the book he wrote about his life. He was more influential in death than during his lifetime. Another spokesman was Huey Newton of the Black Panthers. This organization had guns and said that blacks should defend themselves.

King was growing concerned about problems that the civil rights laws didn't touch—problems of poverty. He also began speaking out against a war the United States was fighting in the Asian nation of Vietnam. King said, "We are spending all of this money for death and destruction, and not nearly enough money for life and constructive development."

The FBI tapped King's private phone conversations, blackmailed him, and threatened him. A U.S. Senate report of 1976 would say that the FBI "tried to destroy Dr. Martin Luther King." But destruction came when an unseen marksman shot King to death as he stood on the balcony outside his hotel room in Memphis, Tennessee.

The killing of King brought new urban violence. African Americans saw that violence and injustice against them continued. Attacks on blacks were endlessly repeated in the history of the United States, coming out of a deep well of racism in the national mind. But there was something more—now the FBI and police were targeting militant black organizers, such as the Black Panthers.

Was the government afraid that black people would turn their attention from issues such as voting to something more dangerous, such as the question of wealth and poverty? If poor whites and blacks united, large-scale class conflict could become a reality.

But if some blacks were invited into the power system, they might turn away from class conflict. So leaders of nonmilitant black groups visited the White House. White-owned banks began helping black businesses. Newspapers and televisions started showing more black faces. These changes were small, but they got a lot of publicity. They also drew some young black leaders into the mainstream.

By 1977, more than two thousand African Americans held public office in southern cities. It was a big advance—but it was still less than 3 percent of all elective offices, although blacks made up 20 percent of the total population.

More blacks could go to universities, to law and medical school. Northern cities were busing children back and forth to integrate their schools. But none of this was helping the unemployment, poverty, crime, drug addiction, and violence that were destroying the black lower class in the ghettos. At the same time, government programs to aid African Americans seemed to favor blacks over whites. When poor whites and poor blacks competed for jobs, housing, and the miserable schools that the government provided for all the poor, new racial tension grew.

No great black movement was under way in the mid-1970s. Yet a new black pride and awareness had been born, and it was still alive. What form would it take in the future?

CHAPTER SIX

VIETNAM

"DEAR MOM AND DAD," AN AMERICAN SOLDIER wrote home from Vietnam, "Today we went on a mission and I am not very proud of myself, my friends, or my country." What kind of war would make a soldier feel that way? It was a war that made many Americans angry and ashamed of their country.

For nearly a decade, the richest and most powerful nation in the history of the world tried to defeat a revolutionary movement in a tiny, peasant country—and failed. When the United States fought a war in the southeastern Asian nation of Vietnam, it was modern military technology against organized human beings. The human beings won.

Vietnam also created the biggest antiwar movement the United States had ever seen. Thousands of people marched in the streets. Students organized protests. Artists, writers, and soldiers boldly spoke out against the war. The antiwar movement was loud and long-lasting. It helped bring the fighting to an end.

Communism and Combat

BEFORE WORLD WAR II, FRANCE CONTROLLED the Southeast Asian nation of Vietnam. When that war started, Japanese troops occupied the country. A revolutionary movement arose among the Vietnamese people, led by a Communist named Ho Chi Minh, to fight the Japanese. At the end of the war, the revolutionaries celebrated in Hanoi, a city in northern Vietnam. A million people filled the streets, rejoicing that their country was free of foreign control at last.

But the Western powers were already taking away that freedom. Before long, England and the United States saw to it that France regained control of Vietnam. Revolutionaries in the north resisted,

and in 1946 the French started bombing them. It
was the beginning of an eight-year war against the
Communist movement, called the Vietminh.
Before it was over, the United States gave a
billion dollars in military aid, along with hundreds
of thousands of weapons, to the French to use
in Vietnam.

Why did the United States help France? The
official reason was to stop the rise of communism
in Asia. Communist governments had already
come to power in China and North Korea. It was
the height of the Cold War, when communism
was seen as the greatest danger to America. But
could there have been other reasons as well?

A secret U.S. government memo from 1952
talked about Southeast Asia's resources. Its rubber, tin, and oil were important to the United
States. If a government that was hostile to the
United States came to power in Vietnam, it might
get in the way of the United States' influence and
interests. In 1954, a memo in the U.S. State
Department said, "If the French actually decided
to withdraw [from Vietnam], the U.S. would have
to consider most seriously whether to take over in
this area."

That same year, the French did withdraw from
northern Vietnam. Under the peace agreement,
the Vietminh agreed to remain in the north. The
northern and southern parts of Vietnam were supposed to be unified after two years, and the people
would be allowed to elect their own government.
It seemed likely that they would choose Ho Chi
Minh and the Vietminh.

The United States moved quickly to keep North
and South Vietnam from being united. To bring
South Vietnam under American influence, it placed
the government in charge of an official named Ngo
Dinh Diem. He was friendly to the United States,
but the Vietnamese people disliked him.

Diem did not hold the scheduled elections.
Around 1958, guerrilla attacks on his government
began in South Vietnam. The guerrillas, called
Viet Cong, were aided by the Communist government of North Vietnam.

The Communist movement gained strength in
the south. To the Vietnamese people, it was more
than a war against Diem. It was a way of reorgan-
izing society so that ordinary villagers would have
more control over their lives. Open opposition to
Diem increased. Buddhist monks set themselves

on fire and burned to death to protest against the South Vietnamese government.

Under the international peace agreement, the United States could send just 685 military advisers to South Vietnam. It sent thousands more, and some of them helped fight against the guerrillas. The United States had entered into a secret, illegal war.

Next, the U.S. administration decided that Diem was not helping them control South Vietnam. The Central Intelligence Agency (CIA) secretly encouraged some Vietnamese generals to overthrow him. The generals attacked Diem's seaside palace and executed him and his brother.

Three weeks later, the American president John F. Kennedy was assassinated in Texas. When his vice president, Lyndon B. Johnson, became president, he inherited the problem of Vietnam.

In August 1964, Johnson told the American public that the North Vietnamese had fired torpedos at a U.S. Navy Ship. It was a lie. The ship had been spying for the CIA in Vietnamese territorial waters, and no torpedoes were fired. But the "attack" gave the United States a reason to make war on North Vietnam. Under the U.S.

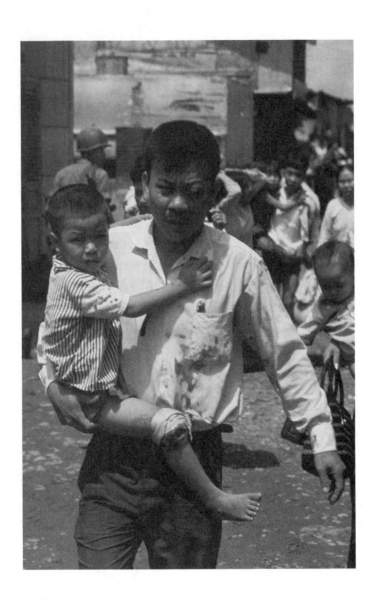

Constitution, only Congress could declare war. Instead, Congress gave the president power to take military actions in Southeast Asia without a formal declaration of war.

American warplanes began bombarding North Vietnam. They also bombed villages in South Vietnam where they thought Viet Cong were hiding. Sometimes they dropped a weapon called napalm, which is gasoline in jelly form, horribly destructive to human flesh. A *New York Times* article from September 1965 described the results:

> In another delta province there is a woman who has both arms burned off by napalm and her eyelids so badly burned that she cannot close them. When it is time for her to sleep her family puts a blanket over her head. The woman had two of her children killed in the air strike that maimed her. Few Americans appreciate what their nation is doing to South Vietnam with airpower. . . . [I]nnocent civilians are dying every day in South Vietnam.

American troops also poured into South Vietnam. By early 1968 there were more than half a million of them there. As they raided villages looking for guerrillas, the difference between an enemy and a civilian seemed to disappear.

(left)
Civilians begin to evacuate homes in Cholon area of Saigon during an attack, 1968.

In March 1968 a company of American soldiers went into a village called My Lai. They rounded up the villagers, including old people and women carrying babies. Then they ordered the people into a ditch and shot them. The army tried to cover up what had happened at My Lai, but after word got out, several of the officers stood trial. A newspaper report of the trial described the massacre at My Lai:

> Lieutenant Calley and a weeping rifleman named Paul D. Meadlo—the same soldier who had fed candy to the children before shooting them—pushed the prisoners into the ditch. . . . People were diving on top of each other; mothers were trying to protect their children. . . . Between 450 and 500 people—mostly women, children, and older men, were buried in mass graves.

Calley was sentenced to life in prison, but he served just three years of house arrest. An army officer admitted that many other tragedies like My Lai remained hidden.

As the war went on, the United States started bombing Laos, Vietnam's neighbor. This was to keep the Viet Cong from operating bases there and to destroy supply routes used by the Viet Cong. The bombing in Laos was kept from the public. But

when the United States later bombed another
Southeast Asian country, Cambodia, the news
reached the public and caused an outcry of protest.

"This Madness Must Cease"

AMERICAN FIREPOWER WAS ENORMOUS, BUT
it wasn't ending the resistance in Vietnam. And in
the United States, the public was turning against
the war. Some were horrified by its cruelty. Others
simply felt that it was a failure that had killed forty
thousand U.S. soldiers and wounded a quarter of
a million more by early 1968.

President Johnson had stepped up a brutal war
and still failed to win it. He became so unpopular
that he could not appear in public without an antiwar demonstration. Protestors shouted, "LBJ, LBJ,
how many kids did you kill today?"

From the start, Americans had protested
against U.S. actions in Vietnam. Some of the first
protests came out of the civil rights movement—
maybe because black people's experience with the

government made them distrust any claim that it was fighting for freedom. In 1965, young blacks in Mississippi who had just learned that a classmate was killed in Vietnam passed out a pamphlet that said: "No Mississippi Negroes should be fighting in Viet Nam for the White man's freedom, until all the Negro People are free in Mississippi."

The Student Nonviolent Coordinating Committee (SNCC), a big part of the civil rights movement, said that the United States was breaking international law in Vietnam. It called for an end to the fighting. When six SNCC members invaded an Alabama induction center (an office for entering the armed forces), they were arrested and sentenced to several years in prison.

Julian Bond, an SNCC activist, was elected to the Georgia legislature. After he spoke out against the war and the draft, the others legislators refused to let him take his seat. The Supreme Court restored Bond to his seat, saying that he had the right to free expression under the First Amendment.

In 1967, Martin Luther King Jr. spoke about the war at Riverside Church in New York:

Somehow this madness must cease. We must stop now. I speak as a child of God and brother to the suffering poor

of Vietnam. I speak for those whose land is being laid
waste, whose homes are being destroyed. . . . I speak
for the poor of America, who are paying the double
price of smashed hopes at home and death and corruption in Vietnam. . . . I speak as an American to the leaders of my own nation. The great initiative in this war is
ours. The initiative to stop it must be ours.

Catholic priests and nuns joined the antiwar
movement. Father Philip Berrigan, a priest who was
also a veteran of World War II, was one of many
people who went to jail for destroying the records at
offices of the draft board, where young men were
required to register for military service. His brother
Daniel, also a priest, was imprisoned for a similar act.

Thousands of young American men fled to
Canada or Europe. Some were avoiding the draft.
Others were soldiers, deserting. Antiwar feeling
was strong among servicepeople, both soldiers
and veterans. Some spoke out, risking punishment. A navy nurse was court-martialed for
marching in a peace demonstration while in uniform. Two black marines went to prison for talking to others against the war.

One antiwar veteran told his story in the book
Born on the Fourth of July. Ron Kovic enlisted in the

U.S. Marines when he was seventeen. He was serving in Vietnam when shellfire shattered his spine and paralyzed him from the waist down. Back in the States, in a wheelchair, Kovic demonstrated against the war. He told how he was treated after being arrested during a demonstration:

"What's your name?" the officer behind the desk says.

"Ron Kovic," I say. "Occupation, Vietnam veteran against the war."

"What?" he says sarcastically, looking down at me.

"I'm a Vietnam veteran against the war," I almost shout back.

"You should have died over there," he says. He turns to his assistant. "I'd like to take this guy and throw him off the roof."

The growth of the antiwar movement couldn't be stopped. When the bombing of North Vietnam had started in 1965, a hundred people gathered in Boston to protest it. But on October 1, 1968, a nationwide day of antiwar activity, a hundred thousand showed up in Boston and as many as 2 million people took part across the United States.

Famous voices and ordinary voices were raised against the war. Arthur Miller, a well-known playwright, was invited to the White House. He

(*left*)
Ron Kovic, 1976.

refused to come. Singer Eartha Kitt did accept an invitation to the White House and shocked everyone by speaking out, in front of the president's wife, against the war. A teenager who had won a prize was called to the White House to accept it. He came—and criticized the war.

Even some of those close to the government had had enough. Daniel Ellsberg, a former U.S. Marine, had helped write a top-secret history of the war for the Department of Defense. He and a friend decided to make it public. They leaked the "Pentagon Papers" to the *New York Times*, which published parts of the document.

By that time, Republican Richard Nixon had replaced Democrat Johnson as president. Nixon tried to get the Supreme Court to stop the *Times* from publishing the Pentagon Papers. He failed. The administration then put Ellsberg and his friend on trial. The trial was halted when unfair and illegal acts by Nixon's own administration—an event called the Watergate scandal—became public.

By the fall of 1973, North Vietnamese troops were established in parts of South Vietnam. The American administration could see no victory in sight. After a final, brutal wave of bombing over the north, the United States signed a peace agreement and withdrew its forces. The South Vietnamese government still received American aid, but without the American military it could not hold off an invasion from North Vietnam. In 1975 the country was united under the Communist rule of Ho Chi Minh.

Vietnam was the first defeat to the global American empire that had formed after World War II. That defeat came from a revolutionary peasant army and from an astonishing movement of protest at home. Yet the rebellion at home was spreading beyond the issue of war in Vietnam.

CHAPTER SEVEN

SURPRISES

"THE TIMES THEY ARE A-CHANGIN'," sang Bob Dylan in the 1960s. Dylan wrote powerful songs of protest. In "Masters of War," he imagined the deaths of the men who organized wars and profited from them. But Dylan also sang personal songs of freedom and self-expression. His music captured the mood of the United States in the 1960s and early 1970s.

It was a time of revolt. The civil rights movement and the movement against the Vietnam War were part of a larger movement for change. People lost faith in the Establishment—the big powers like business, government, the schools, and the medical industry. They questioned what they were told. They believed that they should be free to think for themselves, and they experimented with new ways of living, teaching, working, and making art.

Unexpected new currents began to flow through American society, moving in surprising directions. Two of the biggest surprises came from women and Indians.

Women's Liberation

By 1960, more than a third of all women age sixteen and older were working outside their homes for wages. Yet only 2 percent of working mothers had nurseries for their children, and women earned a lot less than men. Society saw women as wives, mothers, housekeepers. Many men viewed women as emotional and impractical, not able to do difficult jobs.

Even in the civil rights movement, where women played an important role and stood up to danger, some women knew that men did not regard them as equals. Ella Barker, who had worked for civil rights in Harlem before going to the South to help organize protests, said:

> I knew from the beginning that as a woman, an older
> woman in a group of ministers who are accustomed to
> having women largely as supporters, there was no place
> for me to have come into a leadership role.

But women resisted. In 1964, civil rights workers were living in a Freedom House in Mississippi. The women went on strike against the men, who expected them to cook and make beds while the men drove around organizing the movement.

The times *were* a-changing. The National Organization for Women formed in 1966. The following year, women's groups convinced President Johnson to ban discrimination against women in jobs related to the federal government.

By that time, women in the civil rights and anti-war movements were organizing their own meetings and taking action on women's issues. In early 1968 a women's antiwar meeting in Washington, D.C., marched to the Arlington National Cemetery and declared "The Burial of Traditional Womanhood." That same year a group called Radical Women made headlines when they protested the Miss America contest and threw

WOMEN!
hange-SEEK-ACT...
dyssey House
ERA YES
DYSSEYHOUSE
"alk in My Shoes"
Drug-Free
ERA YES
ERA YES
WOMEN

bras, false eyelashes, and wigs into a Freedom Trash Can.

Hoping to change the U.S. Constitution to ensure full equality of the sexes, many women worked to get an Equal Rights Amendment (ERA) passed by the states. Yet it seemed clear that even if they succeeded, the law alone would not be enough to change people's ideas about women's place in society. Shirley Chisholm, a black congresswoman, said:

> The law cannot do it for us. We must do it for ourselves. Women in this country must become revolutionaries. We must refuse to accept the old, the traditional roles and stereotypes. . . . We must replace the old, negative thoughts about our feminity with positive thoughts and positive action. . . .

The women's movement of the 1960s was called Women's Liberation, or sometimes feminism. Its deepest effect might have been what was called "consciousness raising." Women read or talked about issues that affected them. This led them to rethink old roles, to reject the idea that women were inferior, and to feel a new confidence and sense of sisterhood with other women.

(*left*)
Former New York Congresswoman Bella Abzug (2nd from right) joins marchers celebrating the 60th anniversary of the passage of the 19th Amendment to the U.S. Constitution, 1980.

One of the first and most influential books of the women's movement was *The Feminine Mystique,* by a middle-class housewife named Betty Friedan. The "mystique" was society's image of women finding complete satisfaction as mothers and wives, giving up their own dreams. In trying to live up to that image, many women felt empty and lost. Friedan wrote, "The only way for a woman, as for a man, to find herself, to know herself as a person, is by creative work of her own."

Poor women had urgent concerns. Some of them wanted to eliminate hunger, suffering, and inequality right away. Johnnie Tillmon worked with other mothers on welfare to form the National Welfare Rights Organization. It wanted women to be paid for work such as housekeeping and child-rearing, saying, "No woman can be liberated, until all women get off their knees." Tillmon explained:

> Welfare's like a traffic accident. It can happen to anybody, but especially it happens to women. And that is why welfare is a women's issue. For a lot of middle-class women in this country, Women's Liberation is a matter of concern. For women on welfare it's a matter of survival.

The control of women in society was not done by the state. Instead, it happened inside the family. Men controlled women, women controlled children, and sometimes they did violence to each other when things weren't going right. But what if it all turned around?

If women liberated themselves, and men and women began to understand each other, would they find that both of them were being kept down by something outside themselves? Maybe families and relationships would become pockets of strength and rebellion against the larger system, and men and women—and children, too—would work together to change society.

An Indian Uprising

THE INDIANS WERE ONCE THE ONLY INHABITANTS of America. Then the white invaders pushed them back. The last massacre of the Indians took place in 1890 at Wounded Knee Creek in South Dakota. When it was over, between two and three hundred Indian men, women, and children were dead.

The Indian tribes had been attacked, beaten, and starved. The federal government divided them up by putting them on reservations where they lived in poverty. An 1887 law tried to turn the Indians into American-type small farmers by breaking up the reservations into individually owned plots of land. White real-estate speculators got hold of most of the land, and the reservations remained, although young Indians often left them.

For a time, it seemed that the Indians would disappear or blend away into the larger society. At the beginning of the twentieth century, only three hundred thousand of them were left. But then, like a plant that is left to die but refuses to do so, the population started to grow again. By 1960 there were eight hundred thousand Indians. Half of them lived on reservations. The other half lived in cities and towns all over the country.

As the civil rights and antiwar movements took shape in the 1960s, the Indians were also thinking about how to change their situation. They began to organize.

Indians started approaching the U.S. government on an embarrassing topic: treaties. The government had signed more than four hundred

(left) Fear Forgets leads other Sioux in "Liberation Day" ceremonies on Alcatraz Island, 1970.

treaties with the Indians. It had broken every single one. Back when George Washington was president, the government signed a treaty with the Iroquois tribes of New York that gave certain property to the Seneca nation. But in the early 1960s, under President Kennedy, the government ignored that treaty and built a dam on this land, flooding most of the Seneca reservation.

But Indians in all parts of the country were starting to resist. In the state of Washington, an old treaty had taken land from the Indians but left them fishing rights. As the white population grew, whites wanted the fishing to themselves. After state courts closed river areas to Indians, the Indians held "fish-ins" there. They went to jail, hoping to get publicity for their protest.

Some Indians at the fish-ins were Vietnam veterans. One of them was Sid Mills. In 1968, Mills was arrested on the Nisqually River. He said, "I am a Yakima and a Cherokee Indian, and a man. For two years and four months, I've been a soldier in the United States Army. I served in combat in Vietnam—until critically wounded. . . . I hereby renounce further obligation in service or duty to the United States Army."

A dramatic event in 1969 drew more attention to the Indians' complaints than anything else had done. Alcatraz was an abandoned federal prison on an island in San Francisco Bay. It had been a hated place nicknamed "The Rock." One night seventy-eight Indians landed on Alcatraz and took it over.

Among the group's leaders were Richard Oakes, a Mohawk who directed Indian studies at San Francisco State College, and Grace Thorpe, a Sac and Fox Indian who was the daughter of Jim Thorpe, a famous football star and Olympic athlete. Their plan was to turn the island into a center for Native American environmental studies.

Other Indians came to join them. By the end of November there were more than six hundred people from fifty tribes. The government cut off telephone, electric, and water service to the island. Although many Indians had to leave, others insisted on staying. They were still there a year later, when they sent out this message:

> We are still holding the Island of Alcatraz in the true names of Freedom, Justice and Equality, because you, our brothers and sisters of this earth, have lent support to our just cause.

We have learned that violence breeds only more violence
and we have therefore carried on our occupation of
Alcatraz in a peaceful manner, hoping that the government of these United States will also act accordingly...
We are Indians of All Tribes! we hold the rock!

Six months later, federal forces invaded the
island and physically removed the Indians.

Other Indian demonstrations took place—to
protest strip mining on Navajo land in New
Mexico, to reclaim land taken by the Forest
Service in California. At the same time, Indians
were doing something about the destruction of
their culture. An Oklahoma Indian named Evan
Haney recalled that though half the kids in his
school had been Indians, "nothing in school . . .
taught anything about Indian culture. There
were no books on Indian history, not even in
the library. . . ." Haney knew something was
wrong. He found books and started learning his
own culture.

As more books about Indian history came into
being, teachers started to rethink the way they
taught the subject. They avoided old stereotypes
and looked for new sources of information for
their students. Students became activists, too. An

elementary school student named Raymond
Miranda wrote to the publisher of one of his
books:

Dear Editor,

I don't like your book called *The Cruise of Christopher
Columbus*. I didn't like it because you said some things
about Indians that weren't true. . . . Another thing I didn't
like was on page 69, it says that Christopher Columbus
invited the Indians to Spain, but what really happened was
that he stole them!

In March of 1973, the Indians of North America
made a powerful statement on the Pine Ridge
Reservation in South Dakota. Hundreds of
American Indian Movement members occupied
Wounded Knee village at the site of the 1890 massacre. The occupation was a symbol of their
demand for Indian rights and Indian land.

Within hours, federal agents, marshals, and
police surrounded the town. They began firing with
automatic weapons. The protestors inside the town
were under siege. When Indians in Michigan sent
them a small planeload of food, the authorities
arrested the pilot and a doctor who had hired the
plane. A few weeks later other planes dropped food
for the protestors. When the Indians ran to gather

it, a federal helicopter fired down on them. A stray bullet hit a man inside a church. He died.

After more gun battles and another death, the Indians and the authorities agreed to end the siege. A hundred and twenty Indians were arrested. But they had held out for seventy-one days, creating a community inside Wounded Knee and receiving messages of support from all over the world.

The 1960s and early 1970s brought many changes to American society, some large and some small but significant. People felt free to be themselves. Gays and lesbians felt less need to hide the truth about themselves, and they started organizing to fight discrimination. Men and women alike dressed less formally. Comfortable clothes such as jeans became normal for young people of both sexes. Students, parents, and teachers questioned traditional education, which had taught whole generations the values of patriotism and obeying authority while ignoring or even disrespecting women and people of color. Disabled people became a force, campaigning for legislation that would protect them from discrimination.

In those years, as part of what became known as a "cultural revolution," people became more conscious of what was happening to the environment. In 1962 Rachel Carson published *Silent Spring*, a book that shocked people into realizing that chemicals used in modern technology were poisoning the air, the water, and the earth. The book became a bestseller and sparked a movement for environmental cleanliness. In 1978, a woman named Lois Gibbs, whose children had become ill in the neighborhood of Love Canal, New York, and who saw other people suffering, became a leader in the struggle against corporations that were endangering people's lives in their pursuit of maximum profit.

Hundreds of thousands of people joined organizations like the Sierra Club, the Wilderness Society, and EarthFirst! On Earth Day in 1970, 100,000 people marched down Fifth Avenue in New York, and students at 1,500 colleges and 10,000 schools throughout the country demanded protection of the environment. Soon after, Congress passed a number of laws: the Clean Water Act, the Clean Air Act, and the Endangered Species Act. They also created the Environmental

Protection Agency. Enforcement of these acts was not a priority of the national government, and in the presidency of Ronald Reagan, funds were cut for the E.P.A. Nevertheless, the environmental movement continued its campaigns.

America had never had more movements for change in such a short time. But the Establishment had learned a lot about controlling people in its two hundred years of existence. In the mid-1970s, it went to work.

CHAPTER EIGHT

UNDER CONTROL?

"IS THE GOVERNMENT RUN BY A FEW BIG interests looking out for themselves?"

In 1972 a research center asked Americans that question. More than half the people who were asked said, "Yes." Just eight years before, only about a quarter of them had answered yes. What had happened?

America was changing in the early 1970s. The system was out of control. People had lost faith in the government. A lot of them were hostile to big business, too.

The Vietnam War created a lot of distrust and anger. It killed fifty-eight thousand Americans, and the people had discovered that their government had lied to them and had done terrible deeds. Americans also lost faith in the system

because of Watergate, a political disgrace that made a U.S. president step down from office for the first time in history. Many were also deeply concerned about how the United States was acting toward other nations of the world.

Watergate

THE STORY OF WATERGATE BEGAN IN THE White House. Richard M. Nixon, a Republican, was president. To help him win a second term in the White House when voters went to the polls in November, his supporters formed the Committee to Re-Elect the President (CREEP).

Five burglars were caught in Washington, D.C., in June 1972. They were breaking into an office in the Watergate apartment that happened to be the headquarters of the Democratic Party's national committee. Police discovered that the burglars had equipment for taking photographs and wire-tapping telephones. One of them was James McCord Jr., an officer of CREEP. Another burglar

(left)
Newspaper headlines being read by tourists in front of the White House, 1974.

carried an address book. It contained the name E. Howard Hunt and gave Hunt's address as the White House. Hunt, it turned out, worked for Nixon's lawyer.

The burglars weren't just linked to important officials in Nixon's campaign committee and his administration. They also had ties to the country's Central Intelligence Agency. News of the arrests and the burglars' high-level connections got out to the public before anyone could stop it.

Everyone was asking: Did the president have anything to do with the burglary? Did he know about it? Five days after the arrests, Nixon told reporters that "the White House has had no involvement whatever in this particular incident."

But over the next year, a different picture became clear. One after the other, people in the Nixon administration began to talk, sometimes to protect themselves from facing charges. They gave information in court, in meetings of the Senate committee that investigated the Watergate case, and to reporters. They revealed misdeeds by John Mitchell—the attorney general, who is supposed to be the U.S. government's senior lawyer. Also

guilty were two of Nixon's top assistants, Robert
Haldeman and John Ehrlichman. Nixon himself
was deeply involved.

The Watergate burglary wasn't the Nixon
administration's only crime. A long list of facts
came to light. Here are just some of them:

- Attorney General Mitchell had controlled a
  secret fund of hundreds of thousands of dollars
  to use against the Democratic Party. Ways to
  hurt the Democrats inlcuded forging letters,
  stealing campaign files, and leaking false news
  stories to the press.
- Gulf Oil Corporation and other big American
  businesses had given millions of dollars in illegal contributions to Nixon's campaign.
- In September 1971, after the *New York Times*
  started printing the Pentagon Papers, which
  told of U.S. actions in Vietnam, the administration targeted Daniel Ellsberg, who had given
  the Pentagon Papers to the *Times*. Hunt and
  another Nixon supporter had burglarized the
  office of Ellsberg's psychiatrist, looking for
  information to use against Ellsberg.
- Henry Kissinger, Nixon's secretary of state, had
  broken the law by having the telephone calls of

journalists and government officials recorded. Material from this spying was kept in a safe in the White House.

- Nixon had taken an illegal tax deduction of more than half a million dollars.

The list went on and on. Then, while the administration's wrongs were coming to light, the vice president, Spiro Agnew, got into trouble. Agnew was accused of taking bribes in return for political favors. He resigned from his post as vice president in October 1973. Nixon chose a Republican congressman named Gerald Ford to replace him.

But soon Nixon fell from power, too. The House of Representatives was ready to vote on whether or not to impeach, that is, to officially charge him for official misconduct. If that had happened, Nixon would then face a trial in the U.S. Senate. If the Senate convicted Nixon, he would be removed from office. Nixon knew that the House would vote for impeachment and that the Senate would convict him.

Nixon did not wait to be impeached by the House of Representatives. He resigned voluntarily on August 8, 1974. "Our long national nightmare is over," said Gerald Ford, who took Nixon's place as president.

How did the Watergate scandal and the president's resignation affect the government? One businessman said, "What we will have is the same play with different players." A political adviser named Theodore Sorensen said something similar: "All the rotten apples should be thrown out. But save the barrel."

The barrel—the system—was saved. Big business and powerful corporations still had great influence in Washington under President Ford. Whether Nixon or Ford or any Republican or Democrat was president, the system would work pretty much the same way. The power of corporations on the White House is a fact of the American political system, and that didn't change after Watergate. The companies that had made illegal contributions to Nixon's campaigns got very light punishment—tiny fines, much smaller than the millions they had given.

America Overseas

MANY SECRETS CAME TO LIGHT DURING
the Watergate investigation. One of them involved
Cambodia, a Southeast Asian country next to
Vietnam. In 1969–1970, the United States had
dropped thousands of bombs on Cambodia. The
bombing of Cambodia was part of the Vietnam
War, but it was concealed from the American public and even from Congress. When it was revealed,
it fed people's doubts about the government's foreign policy.

Foreign policy is how a country's government
acts toward other nations. For a long time, U.S.
foreign policy was focused on fighting in Vietnam.
But that war became unpopular with the
American people, and after it ended, some government and business leaders feared that the public
might not support other military actions overseas.

Henry Kissinger worried about that very
thing. Kissinger continued to serve as U.S. secretary of state under President Ford. In April
1975 he was supposed to give a speech at the
University of Michigan. Many students were
unhappy about this because of Kissinger's role
in the Vietnam War. They protested so strongly

that he decided not to come. It was a low time for the administration. How could the government improve its image?

"The U.S. must carry out some act somewhere in the world which shows its determination to continue to be a world power," Kissinger said. The next month, the United States seized a chance to make that statement of power.

An American cargo ship called the *Mayaguez* was sailing near Tang Island. The island is part of Cambodia, where a revolutionary government had just taken power. Cambodians stopped the ship and took its crew to the mainland. The crew later said that they were treated with courtesy.

President Ford sent a message to Cambodia to release the ship and crew. After thirty-six hours, U.S. planes started bombing Cambodian ships—even the boat that was carrying the American sailors. Soon Cambodia released the Americans, but Ford had already ordered an attack on Tang Island, even though he knew the soldiers weren't there.

Forty-one Americans were killed in the attack on Tang Island. Why the rush to bomb? And why did Ford order the Cambodian mainland bombed, even after the *Mayaguez* and the crew were recovered?

Why? To show the world that the giant America, defeated by tiny Vietnam, was still powerful. But many journalists and television reporters called the *Mayaguez* operation "successful" and "efficient." The Establishment, it seemed, stood behind the idea that America should shown its authority everywhere in the world. This was true of both liberals and conservatives, Democrats and Republicans.

Congress acted in the *Mayaguez* affair just as it had acted in the early years of the Vietnam War—like a flock of sheep. In 1973, disgusted with Vietnam, Congress had passed a law called the War Powers Act. This law said that the president must consult with Congress before taking military action. But in the *Mayaguez* affair, Ford ignored the law. His assistants called eighteen members of Congress to tell them about the military action. Only a few protested.

Watergate had made both the Central Intelligence Agency and the Federal Bureau of Investigation (FBI) look bad. Those agencies had broken the laws they were sworn to uphold, and they had helped Nixon with illegal acts. When Congress set up committees to study the CIA and

(left)
Part of a Cambodian task force attempting to clear Route 7 east of Skoun watches as American air support bombs Communist positions nearby, 1970.

the FBI after Watergate, it found even more dirty secrets.

The CIA had been plotted to assassinate the leaders of foreign nations, such as Cuba's Fidel Castro. It had smuggled a livestock disease into Cuba that destroyed half a million pigs belonging to people on the island. The CIA had also worked to upset the government of Chile. That government was headed by Salvador Allende, a Marxist. He had been freely elected by the people of Chile—but the United States disagreed with his politics.

As for the FBI, it had spent years trying to break up and destroy left-wing and radical groups. It sent forged letters, it opened mail illegally, and it performed more than ninety burglaries in just six years alone. The FBI even seems to have taken part in the murder of Fred Hampton, an African American activist in the Black Panthers.

All of this information reached the public in thick, hard-to-read reports. Television reporters did not say much about it, and the newspapers did not give full coverage. The Senate even let the CIA review its report *about* the CIA, in case the report had information that the CIA did not want people to read! So that while the investigations made it look as if an honest society was fixing its problems, the mass media and the government did nothing to encourage an open, public discussion of those problems.

Nixon stepping down as president . . . Congress looking into bad deeds by the CIA and the FBI . . . these things were supposed to win back the confidence of the American people in their government. Did they work?

A poll in 1975 found that people's confidence in the military, in buisiness, and in government had plunged since 1966. Only 13 percent of people said that they had confidence in the president and Congress.

Maybe people's lack of satisfaction had something to do with the economy. Unemployment was rising. People were losing their jobs and running out of unemployment benefits. More and more Americans were feeling worse about the future.

In the year 1976, with a presidential election on the way, the Establishment worried about the public's faith in the system. That year was also the bicentennial, or two-hundredth anniversary, of the Declaration of Independence. A great celebration was planned. Organizers might have thought that it would bring back American patriotism and end the mood of protest that had developed since the 1960s.

But there didn't seem to be much enthusiasm for the Bicentennial. In Boston, a 200th anniversary of the Boston Tea Party was planned. But a huge crowd turned out at an unofficial "counter-celebration," where people dumped boxes into Boston Harbor. Marked "Gulf Oil" and "Exxon," those boxes were symbols of corporate power in America. The mood of protest had not gone away.

CHAPTER NINE

POLITICS AS USUAL

TEN MILLION CHILDREN WHO LIVED IN THE
United States in 1979 might not have been able to
go to the doctor or get medicine when they were
sick. That's because they had no known source of
regular health care. Eighteen million kids under
the age of seventeen had never been to a dentist.

Marian Wright Edelman pointed out these
facts. She was the head of the Children's Defense
Fund, working to make life better for America's
children, especially those who lived in poverty. She
wanted people to know about the holes in the
safety net that was supposed to protect kids,
because the U.S. Congress had just taken $88 mil-
lion away from a children's health program.

The United States was in the grip of serious
problems. The Vietnam War and the Watergate

scandal had made many people distrust the government. A lot of them also worried about money: Would they have enough to support them and their families in the future? Would they slide into poverty? The environment was another concern, as people became aware of dangers such as air and water pollution.

Only bold changes in the social and economic structure could solve these problems. But none of the politicians from the two major parties, Republican or Democrat, suggested big changes. Instead, both parties stayed true to what historian Richard Hofstadter has called "the American political tradition."

Two big parts of that tradition are capitalism and nationalism. The economic system of capitalism encourages the growth of great fortunes alongside desperate poverty. Nationalism, the belief that the interests of the United States must always come first around the world, encourages war and preparations for war. Toward the end of the twentieth century, government power swung back and forth between Democrats and Republicans, but neither party offered a new vision of how things could be.

A Little Bit to the Left

JIMMY CARTER, A DEMOCRAT, WAS PRESIDENT from 1977 to 1980. He moved America toward the left, toward liberalism—but only a little. In spite of some gestures toward black people and the poor, and talk about human rights in the rest of the world, the Carter presidency stayed within the limits of traditional American politics.

Carter named Andrew Young, a black man who had worked in the civil-rights movement, as the U.S. ambassador to the United Nations. In the black nations of Africa, Young built up goodwill for the United States. The Carter administration also urged the white-ruled nation of South Africa to end apartheid, a system of laws that kept blacks from gaining economic or political equality.

The black fight against apartheid had plunged South Africa into disorder. If that disorder turned into all-out civil war, American interests could be threatened. Radar systems in South Africa helped track the planes and satellites of many nations, and the country was a source of important raw materials, especially diamonds, which are used in industry as well as in jewelry. If the United States took a stand against apartheid because it was

morally wrong, America also had practical reasons for wanting a stable, peaceful South Africa.

During the Vietnam War, Carter had presented himself as a friend of the antiwar movement. But Carter had not opposed President Nixon's bombing attacks, and when the war ended, he refused to give aid to help Vietnam rebuild itself. As president, Carter continued U.S. support for oppressive governments in Iran, Nicaragua, the Philippines, and Indonesia. These governments allowed the use of harsh and undemocratic methods—such as torture and mass murder—against political dissidents. Still, they received American aid, including military aid.

If Carter's job was to restore public faith in the system, his greatest failure was that he did not solve people's economic problems. While the military budget remained enormous, the government saved money in other ways. The Department of Agriculture, for example, said that it would save $25 million a year by no longer giving free second helpings of milk to needy schoolchildren.

The price of food and other necessary goods was rising faster than people's wages. Many people didn't even earn wages. Among young people,

(left)
Jimmy Carter, the thirty-ninth president of the United States, 1976.

especially young black people, 20 to 30 percent could not find jobs.

Wealth and Poverty in America

IN 1980, CARTER LOST THE PRESIDENTIAL election to Republican Ronald Reagan. The faint liberalism of the Carter years was gone. After two terms as president, Reagan would be followed by another Republican, George Bush.

The Reagan and Bush administrations followed similar policies. These included cutting benefits to poor people, lowering taxes for the rich, and raising the military budget. The two administrations also filled the federal court system with conservative judges who would interpret the law in ways that favored right-wing, Establishment interests. For example, the Reagan-Bush Supreme Court brought back the death penalty. It also said that poor people could be forced to pay for public education.

During Reagan's first four years as president,

the U.S. military was given more than a trillion dollars. Reagan tried to pay for this by cutting benefits to the poor. The human costs of these cuts went deep. More than a million children lost free school lunches, even though some of those kids depended on school lunches for more than half of their daily nutrition. Aid to Families with Dependent Children (AFDC), a welfare program that provided money for single mothers, came under attack, too. Soon a quarter of the nation's children—twelve million kids—were living in poverty.

One mother wrote to her local newspaper:

I am on Aid to Families with Dependent Children, and both my children are in school. . . .

It appears we have employment offices that can't employ, governments that can't govern and an economic system that can't produce jobs for people ready to work. . . .

Last week I sold my bed to pay for the insurance on my car, which, in the absence of mass transportation, I need to go job hunting. I sleep on a piece of rubber foam somebody gave me.

So this is the great American Dream my parents came to this country for: Work hard, get a good education, follow the rules, and you will be rich. I don't want to be rich. I just

want to be able to feed my children and live with some
semblance of dignity. . . .

With strong ties to wealthy corporations, both
the Democratic and Republican political parties
criticized welfare programs. But how did the general public feel about helping those less fortunate?

A poll in early 1992 showed that when questioned about "welfare," 44 percent of people said
that too much money was being spent on it. But
when questioned about "assistance to the poor,"
only 13 percent thought too much was being
spent, and 64 percent thought not enough was
being spent. Americans, it seemed, still felt gener-
ous to those in need, but "welfare" had become a
political term, so people's answers depended upon
how the question was worded.

During the Reagan years, the gap between rich
and poor in the United States grew dramatically.
In 1980, the top officers of corporations made
forty times as much in salary as the average factory worker. By 1989 they were making ninety-
three times as much.

On the lower levels of society, everyone was
doing worse than they had been. Blacks,
Hispanics, women, and the young suffered espe-

cially severe economic hurts. At the end of the 1980s, at least a third of African American families fell below the official poverty level. Unemployment among blacks was much higher than among whites, and life expectancy was lower. The victories of the civil rights movement had made it possible for some African Americans to move ahead, but left others far behind.

Desert Storm

THE MOST DRAMATIC TURN IN INTERNATIONAL affairs since the end of World War II happened early in the presidency of George Bush. In 1989, protests against dictatorship broke out in the Soviet Union and the Eastern European nations controlled by the Soviet Union.

Almost overnight, it seemed, the old Communist governments fell apart. New non-Communist ones came into being. The wall that had divided democratic West Germany from Communist East Germany was torn down in front of wildly cheering citizens. Most remarkable of all, these things happened without civil war, in response to overwhelming demand from the people.

The sudden collapse of the Soviet Union left U.S. political leaders unprepared. Several trillion dollars had been taken from American taxpayers to pay for a huge military buildup all over the world to defend the United States from the "Soviet threat." Now the threat was gone. It was a chance for the United States to create a new foreign policy. Hundreds of billions of dollars could be freed from the military budget to pay for constructive, healthful projects.

But that didn't happen. There was a kind of panic, as leaders wondered what they could do to keep up the military establishment that had cost so many dollars over so many years. As if to prove that the gigantic military force was still needed, the Bush administration started two wars in four years.

The first war was in Panama, in Central America, where General Manuel Noriega ruled as dictator. For years the United States had overlooked Noriega's corrupt and brutal ways because he went along with the U.S. Central Intelligence Agency in many ways. But once Noriega was openly known as a drug trafficker, his usefulness was over.

The United States invaded Panama in December 1989, saying that it wanted Noriega to stand trial for drug crimes. American troops quickly captured Noriega, who went to trial and then to prison in the United States. But the U.S. bombing of Panamanian neighborhoods killed hundreds, perhaps thousands, of civilians and left fourteen thousand homeless.

If Panama was a "small" war, Bush's second war was massive. In August 1990, the Middle Eastern nation of Iraq invaded its smaller neighbor, oil-rich Kuwait. On October 30, the Bush administration made a secret decision to make war on Iraq.

The American people were told that the war was being fought to free Kuwait from the Iraqis and to keep Iraq from developing a nuclear bomb. In reality, the two main reasons for going to war were to give the United States a greater voice in the control of Middle East oil and to boost Bush's chances of reelection by showing that he could win a war on foreign soil.

For months, the government and the major media lectured the public about the danger from

Saddam Hussein, the brutal dictator of Iraq. Even so, less than half the American public favored the idea of war. That did not prevent the administration from sending half a million men to the Persian Gulf, next to Iraq.

In January 1991, Congress gave Bush the authority to make war. Air attacks on Iraqi forces began. Bush called the war Desert Storm. News about the fighting was tightly controlled by the military and the government. The big story of the war was "smart bombs," weapons guided by lasers. These bombs were supposedly so accurate that military targets could be pinpointed, saving civilian lives.

The public was deceived about how "smart" these bombs really were. Thousands of Iraqi civilians, including women and children, died in the bombings, especially after the U.S. Air Force went back to using ordinary bombs. One Egyptian witness described the attack on a hotel south of the Iraqi capital of Baghdad this way: "They hit the hotel, full of families, and then they came back to hit it again."

The war lasted barely six weeks. Afterward, it was clear that the bombings of Iraq had caused

(left)
U.S. troops stationed in Saudi Arabia during the Gulf War, 1991.

starvation, disease, and the deaths of thousands of children. And although the U.S. government had painted Saddam Hussein as a grave danger in the months leading up to the war, at the end of the war he remained in power. The United States had wanted to weaken him, but not get rid of him, it seemed. Hussein had been useful in the past, keeping the neighboring nation of Iran from becoming too powerful in the region, and he might be useful again.

President Bush and the major media cheered the U.S. victory in Desert Storm. They claimed that the lingering ghost of Vietnam and the bitter failure to win the war there were finally laid to rest. The United States had showed the rest of the world what it could do.

But June Jordan, a black poet in California, had a different view. She compared the joy of victory in war to the effect of a deadly drug, saying, "I suggest to you it's a hit the same way that crack is, and it doesn't last long."

CHAPTER TEN

RESISTANCE

A YOUNG ACTIVIST NAMED KEITH MCHENRY was arrested time and time again in the early 1990s. So were hundreds of other people. What was their crime? Giving free food to poor people— without a license to distribute food.

McHenry and others like him were part of a program called Food Not Bombs. Their acts of courage and defiance helped keep alive a spirit of resistance at a time when the power of corporate wealth and government authority seemed overwhelming.

In the 1960s, the surge of protest against race segregation and against war had become a powerful national force. The resistance of the late 1970s, the 1980s, and the early 1990s was different. Activists struggled uphill against uncaring political leaders. They tried hard to reach their fellow Americans, even though many people saw little hope in either voting or protest.

Politicians mostly ignored this resistance. The major media didn't mention it very often. But thousands of local groups were busy around the country. Activists in these groups worked for the environment, women's rights, housing for the homeless, and an end to military spending.

No More Nukes!

THE MOVEMENT AGAINST NUCLEAR WEAPONS started in the late 1970s, when Jimmy Carter was president. It was small but determined. Christian activists who had protested the Vietnam War were the pioneers of the movement. They were arrested for nonviolent but dramatic acts at the White House and the Pentagon, the nation's military headquarters. They trespassed on forbidden areas and poured their own blood on symbols of the war machine.

More people joined the antinuclear movement in the 1980s as a protest against President Ronald Reagan's huge military budget. Women took a leading role. Shortly after Reagan was elected, two thousand women gathered in Washington, D.C. They marched on the Pentagon and surrounded it. A hundred and forty of them were arrested for blocking the entrance.

A few doctors started teaching the public about the medical harm that nuclear war would bring. They formed Physicians for Social Responsibility. The group's leader, Dr. Helen Caldicott, became one of the movement's most powerful spokespeople.

Scientists who had worked on the atomic bomb added their voices to the antinuclear movement. Just before he died of cancer, one scientist urged people to organize "a mass movement for peace such as there has not been before."

A mass meeting such as there had not been before took place in New York City's Central Park on June 12, 1982. Close to a million people gathered to call for an end to the arms race, which had the United States and the Soviet Union racing to build up stockpiles of deadly weapons. It was the largest political demonstration in American history.

Social Issues

THE ARMS RACE WASN'T THE ONLY THING THAT
sparked protest. People reacted angrily to Reagan's
cuts in social services. In 1981, people who lived in
East Boston took to the streets to protest the loss
of government money to pay for teachers, police,
and firefighters in their community. For fifty-five
days they blocked major streets during rush hour.
The *Boston Globe* reported that the protestors were
"mostly middle-aged, middle- or working-class
people who said they had never protested anything
before." Said Boston's chief of police, "Maybe
these people are starting to take lessons from the
protests of the sixties and seventies."

Many people saw a link between the nation's
military policy and its failing system of social welfare. Money was being spent on guns instead of
on children. In 1983 Marian Wright Edelman of
the Children's Defense Fund made a speech to a
graduating class of students. She said:

> You are graduating into a nation and world teetering on
> the brink of moral and economic bankruptcy. Since 1980,
> our President and Congress have been . . . bringing good
> news to the rich at the expense of the poor. . . . Children
> are the major victims.

(left)
Marion Wright
Edelman, president
of the Children's
Defense Fund, 1985.

RESISTANCE

In the South, there was no great movement like the civil rights movement of the 1960s. Still, hundreds of local groups organized poor people, black and white. In North Carolina, a woman named Linda Stout, whose father had been killed by industrial poisons, started the Piedmont Peace Project. Its members were hundreds of textile workers, maids, and farmers. Many of them were low-income women of color who found a voice through the group.

Latinos (Americans of Mexican or Latin American descent) also raised their voices against injustice. Back in the 1960s, Mexican American farmworkers led by César Chávez had taken action against unfair and oppressive working conditions. They went on strike and organized a national boycott, urging customers not to buy California grapes until the workers received better treatment.

Latinos' struggles against poverty and discrimination continued in the 1970s and 1980s. Copper miners in Arizona, mostly Latinos, went on strike after the company that owned the mines cut their wages, benefits, and safety protection. The striking miners were attacked by state troopers, tear gas, and helicopters, but they held out for three years. Finally a combination of government and corporate power defeated them and ended the strike.

But there were victories, too. Latino farmworkers, janitors, and factory workers gained pay raises and better working conditions through labor strikes. In New Mexico, Latinos fought real-estate developers to keep the land they had lived on for decades—and won. By this time 12 percent of Americans were Latino, the same percentage as for African Americans. The Latino population would keep growing, and it would begin to make its mark on American music, art, language, and culture.

War and Antiwar

THE VIETNAM WAR HAD ENDED IN 1975. Sometimes, though, it came back into public attention in the 1980s and 1990s. This could happen when someone announced a change in thinking about the war.

One person whose ideas turned completely

around was Charles Hutto, a soldier who had been part of the massacre at the Vietnamese village of My Lai, where U.S. troops shot hundreds of women and children. Looking back, Hutto told a reporter:

> I was nineteen years old, and I'd always been told to do what the grown-ups told me to do. . . . But now I'll tell my sons, if the government calls, to go, to serve their country, but to use their own judgment at times . . . to forget about authority . . . to use their own conscience. I wish some-body had told me that before I went to Vietnam. I didn't know. Now I don't even think there should be a thing called war . . . cause it messes up a person's mind.

Many Americans felt that Vietnam had been a terrible tragedy, a war that should not have been fought. After that hard lesson, people would not automatically support a new war just because the Establishment wanted to fight it. That's why President George Bush launched the air war against Iraq in 1991 with overwhelming force. He wanted the war to be over before a national anti-war movement could form.

But resistance and protest started in the months leading up to the war. Six hundred students marched through Missoula, Montana, shouting

(left)
Protest against the Gulf War, 1991.

antiwar slogans. In Boston, a group called Veterans for Peace joined the annual Veterans Day parade. Onlookers applauded when they walked past carrying signs that read "No More Vietnams."

As Bush moved toward war, Vietnam veteran Ron Kovic, author of *Born on the Fourth of July*, made a speech that was broadcast on two hundred television stations. Kovic urged citizens to "stand up and speak out" against war. He said, "How many more Americans coming home in wheelchairs—like me—will it take before we learn?"

On the night the war began, five thousand protestors gathered in San Francisco and formed a human chain around the Federal Building. Police broke the chain by swinging clubs at the protestors' hands. On the other side of the country, in Boston, a seven-year-old girl made her voice heard, too. She wrote a letter:

> Dear President Bush. I don't like the way you are behaving. If you would make up your mind there won't be a war we won't have to have peace vigils. If you were in a war you wouldn't want to get hurt. What I'm saying is: I don't want any fighting to happen.

Once the fighting started, and patriotic messages filled the media, the majority of Americans said they supported the war. Still, some people courageously spoke out against it.

In the 1960s, Julian Bond had been kicked out of the seat he had been elected to fill in the Georgia Legislature for daring to criticize the Vietnam War. In that same room, Representative Cynthia McKinnon made a speech attacking the bombing of Iraq. Many of her fellow lawmakers walked out, refusing to listen, but she held her ground.

Patricia Biggs was a student at East Central Oklahoma State University. She and another young woman sat quietly on top of the school's entrance gate with signs that read, "Teach Peace . . . Not War." Biggs explained:

> I don't think we should be over there [in Iraq]. I don't think it's about justice and liberty, I think it's about economics. The big oil corporations have a lot to do with what is going on over there. . . . We are risking people's lives for money.

Nine days after the war started, more than 150,000 people marched through the streets of Washington, D.C., and listened to antiwar speeches. A woman from Oakland, California, held up the folded American flag that had been given to her when her husband was killed in

Vietnam. She told the crowd, "I learned the hard way that there is no glory in a folded flag."

The Iraq War lasted just six weeks. Right after it ended, patriotic fever was high. In one poll, only 17 percent of people said that the war had not been worth its huge cost. But four months later, 30 percent felt the war had not been worth it. The war had not won Bush the lasting support of the people. He ran for reelection in 1992, after the war spirit had faded away, and lost.

Remembering Columbus

THE YEAR 1992 WAS THE QUINCENTENNIAL, or five-hundredth anniversary, of Christopher Columbus' arrival in the Americas. Columbus and his fellow conquerors had wiped out the Native American peoples of Hispaniola. Later, the United States government had destroyed Indian tribes as it marched across North America. As the quincentennial approached, the surviving Indians were determined to have their say.

In 1990 Indians from all over the Americas met in Ecuador, South America, to organize against the celebrations that were being planned to honor Columbus' conquest. Two years later, during the quincentennial, other Americans joined them in speaking out against Columbus.

For the first time in all the years that the United States had celebrated Columbus Day, there were nationwide protests against honoring a man who had kidnapped, enslaved, and murdered the Native people who had greeted him with gifts and friendship. All over the country, people held counter-Columbus events.

The Columbus controversy sparked a burst of activity in universities and schools. Traditional or mainstream thinkers saw American history as the progress of European culture into a wilderness. They were upset by the movement to look at history in new ways, to tell the stories of the Indians Columbus had murdered, the blacks who had been denied freedom, and the women who had had to fight for equality. But they could not stop the tide of new thinking.

Socially conscious teachers created books and workshops for other teachers. They encouraged educators to tell their students the truths about Columbus that were left out of traditional textbooks. One student, a girl named Rebecca, had this to say about the traditional teachings:

> Of course, the writers of the books probably think it's harmless enough—what does it matter who discovered America, really. . . . But the thought that I have been lied to all my life about this, and who knows what else, really makes me angry.

Rebecca was not the only angry American. As the United States entered the 1990s, the political system was in the control of the very rich. Corporations owned the major media. The country was divided into extreme wealth and extreme poverty, separated by a middle class that felt troubled and insecure. Yet a culture of protest and resistance survived. Some people refused to give up the vision of a more equal, more human society. If there was hope for the future of America, it lay with them.

CHAPTER ELEVEN

THE END OF
THE TWENTIETH CENTURY

EACH YEAR SOMEONE WINS THE NOBEL PEACE
Prize for seeking a peaceful solution to one of the
world's problems. In 1996 the prize went to two
men who were working to find a fair way to end a
war in East Timor, an Asian country that was
fighting for independence from Indonesia.

Before receiving the prize, one of those men,
Jose Ramos-Horta, spoke at a church in Brooklyn,
New York. He recalled a visit to America almost
twenty years earlier:

> In the summer of 1977, I was here in New York when I
> received a message telling me that one of my sisters,
> Maria, twenty-one years old, had been killed in an aircraft
> bombing. The aircraft, named Bronco, was supplied by
> the United States. . . . Within months, a report about a
> brother, Guy, seventeen years old, killed along with many

other people in his village by Bell helicopters supplied by the United States. Same year, another brother, Nunu, captured and executed with an [American-made] M-16.

Why were American weapons killing people in East Timor, a country on the far side of the world, when the United States was not at war there? Because the United States gave military aid to Indonesia. Toward the end of the twentieth century, the United States became the world's leading provider of weapons to other nations. At the same time, it continued to build up its own military machine.

Military spending took money away from social programs. Dwight Eisenhower, who was president in the middle of the twentieth century, had known that. In one of his best moments, Eisenhower said, "Every gun that is made, every warship launched, every rocket fired, [means] a theft from those who are hungry and are not fed, those who are cold and are not clothed."

During the 1990s, under the eight-year presidency of Bill Clinton, the United States continued to be a place where some people were hungry and cold. It remained a nation where one-fourth of all children lived in poverty and homeless people huddled in the streets of every major city. The country's leaders did not look for bold solutions to the problems of health care, education, child care, unemployment, housing, and the environment.

Moving Toward the Middle

CLINTON WAS A SMART, YOUNG DEMOCRAT in 1992, when Americans elected him to his first term as president. He promised to bring change to the country, and his presidency began with that hope. Upon his reelection in 1996, Clinton declared, "We need a new government for a new century."

But during eight years in office, Clinton failed to live up to his promise of change. Instead, he delivered more of what the country had gotten from the presidents before him.

Like other politicians, Clinton seemed to be more interested in getting votes than in bringing about social change. To win votes, he decided to move the Democratic Party closer to the center—

THE END OF THE TWENTIETH CENTURY

in other words, to make the party less liberal and more conservative, so that it would not be too different from the Republican Party. To do this, he had to do just enough for the blacks, women, and working people who had traditionally been Democrats to keep their support. At the same time, he tried to win over white conservative voters by coming out in favor of welfare cuts and a strong military.

Even before he was elected, Clinton was eager to show that he took a tough position on matters of "law and order." As governor of Arkansas, he flew back to his home state for the execution of a mentally retarded man on death row.

Soon after he became president, Clinton approved an attack by the Federal Bureau of Investigation (FBI) on a group of religious extremists who had sealed themselves up, with weapons, inside a group of buildings in Waco, Texas. Instead of waiting to see if the crisis could be solved through talking, the FBI attacked with rifle fire, tanks, and tear gas, killing at least eighty-six men, women, and children.

In 1996, Republicans and Democrats in Congress voted in favor of a new law called a

166

"Crime Bill." Clinton supported the bill, which made more crimes punishable by death. It also set aside $8 billion of federal money to build new prisons. Throughout his presidency Clinton chose federal judges whose liberalism was of the mild, middling kind. Often their decisions were just like those of more conservative judges.

Clinton was no different from other people in power, whether Democrats or Republicans. To keep themselves in power, they turned the public's anger toward groups that could not defend themselves. The target could be criminals, immigrants, people on welfare, or certain governments hostile to the United States, such as Iraq or Communist Cuba. By urging people to focus on these sources of possible danger, political leaders drew attention away from the failures of the American system.

Choices

THE UNITED STATES WAS THE RICHEST COUNTRY in the world. With 5 percent of the world's population, it used or ate or bought 30 percent of everything that was produced worldwide. But only a tiny fraction of Americans benefited from the country's great wealth.

Starting in the late 1970s, the richest 1 percent of people in the country saw their wealth grow enormously. Changes in the tax laws meant that by 1995, that richest 1 percent had gained more than a trillion dollars. It owned 40 percent of the country's wealth. Between 1982 and 1995, the wealth of the four hundred richest families in the country had jumped from $92 billion to $480 billion. In the same time period, the cost of living rose faster than the average wage of ordinary working people. People earning an average wage could buy about 15 percent *less* in 1995 than in 1982.

If you looked just at the richest part of the American population, you could say the economy was healthy. Meanwhile, 40 million people had no health insurance. Babies and young children in the United States died of sickness and malnutrition at a higher rate than in any other industrial country. Jobs weren't always the answer. In 1998, a third of all working people in the country didn't earn enough to lift them above the government's official poverty level. Many people who worked in factories, stores, or restaurants couldn't afford housing, health care, or even enough food.

Two sources of money were available to pay for social programs to attack poverty, joblessness, and other national problems.

The first source was the military budget. One expert on military spending suggested that gradually lowering the country's military budget to $60 million a year would fit the country's needs, now that the Soviet Union had collapsed and the Cold War had ended.

A big drop in the military budget would have meant closing U.S. military bases around the world. It would have meant that the nation would turn its back on war. The basic human desire of people to live in peace with one another would guide its foreign policy. That was a choice that didn't get made. The military budget kept rising. By the end of Clinton's presidency, military spending was about $300 billion a year.

The second source of money for social programs was the wealth of the superrich. A "wealth tax" could have added $100 billion a year to the nation's treasury. Clinton did raise the tax rate on the superrich and on corporations, but only slightly. It was a pitifully small step compared with the nation's needs.

Together, cuts in the military budget and higher taxes on the superrich could have given the government as much as $500 billion each year to pay for dramatic changes. This money could have paid for health care for everyone and for programs to create jobs for all. Instead of giving out contracts for companies to build bombers and nuclear submarines, the government could have given contracts to nonprofit agencies to hire people to build homes, clean up rivers, and construct public transportation systems.

Instead, things continued as before. Cities kept falling into disrepair. Farmers were forced off their land by debts. Young people without jobs or hope turned to drugs and crime. The response of the government was to build more jails and lock up more people. By the end of the Clinton years, the United States had more than 2 million people in prison—a higher percentage of the population than any other country in the world, except maybe Communist China.

Visions of Change

CLINTON CLAIMED THAT HIS DECISIONS WERE based on the opinion of the American people. But opinion surveys in the 1980s and 1990s showed that Americans favored health care for everyone. They also were in favor of guaranteed jobs, government help for the poor and homeless, military budget cuts, and taxes on the rich. Neither the Republicans nor the Democrats were willing to take these bold steps.

What if the American people acted on the feelings they showed in those surveys? What if citizens organized to demand what the Declaration of Independence promised: a government that protected the equal rights of all to life, liberty, and the pursuit of happiness? This would call for an economic system that distributed wealth in a thoughtful and humane way. It would mean a culture where young people were not taught to seek success as a mask for greed.

Throughout the Clinton years, many Americans did protest government policy. They demanded a more fair and peaceful society. They did not get much attention in the media, though. Even a gathering of half a million children and

adults, of all colors, who came to the nation's capital to "Stand for the Children" was mostly ignored by television and newspapers. Still, activists for peace, women's rights, and racial equality continued their struggle—and won some victories.

The labor movement was alive, too. A protest at Harvard University in Massachusetts showed how different groups could work together to reach a goal.

Many of Harvard's janitors and other campus workers did not earn enough to support themselves and their families. Some had to work two jobs, as much as eighty hours a week. So students organized to demand that the workers be paid a "living wage."

The students staged rallies to win support for their cause. Local city council members and union leaders took part. Two young movie stars, Matt Damon and Ben Affleck, also showed up to speak in favor of a living wage. Damon had attended Harvard before going to Hollywood. Affleck told how his father had worked at a poorly paid service job at Harvard.

When university administrators refused to talk with the campus workers, students took over an administration building and stayed in it day and

(*left*)
The police confront the anti-WTO demonstrators, 1999.

night for several weeks, supported by hundreds of people outside and by donations from all over the country. Finally the university agreed to raise workers' pay and give them health benefits. Soon students and workers were organizing living wage movements at other schools.

In 1999 a great gathering of demonstrators met in Seattle, Washington. They wanted to show the people of America and the world how the power of giant multinational corporations controls the lives of ordinary people.

The World Trade Organization (WTO) was meeting in Seattle. Representatives of the world's richest and most powerful companies and countries were there to make plans to maintain their wealth and power. Their goal was to bring the principles of capitalism to work everywhere, through free-trade agreements between nations.

Protestors claimed that free-trade agreements would let corporations roam the globe looking for cheap labor and places where they could operate without strict environmental laws. The issues of free trade are complicated, but protestors asked a simple question: Should the health and freedom of ordinary people all over the world be sacrificed so that corporations can make a profit?

Tens of thousands of demonstrators showed up to march, make speeches, and carry signs. They were labor unionists, women's rights activists, farmers, environmentalists, consumers, religious groups, and more. The media focused on the small number of demonstrators who broke windows and created trouble, but the overwhelming majority of demonstrators were nonviolent.

Hundreds were jailed, but the protests continued. News of them traveled all over the world. The WTO talks collapsed, showing that organized citizens can challenge the most powerful corporations of the world. Mike Brannan, writing for a union newspaper, captured the protestors' mood:

> The kind of solidarity that all of us dream of was in the air as people sang, chanted, played music, and stood up to the cops and the WTO. The people owned the streets that day and it was as much a lesson for us as it was for corporate America.

Protestors started showing up wherever meetings of the rich and powerful took place. Large international organizations such as the World Bank and the International Monetary Fund could not ignore the movement. They started talking about concern for the environment and for working conditions. Would this lead to real change? It was too soon to tell, but at least the voices of protest had been heard.

CHAPTER TWELVE

THE "WAR ON TERRORISM"

"I DON'T THINK THEY CARE ABOUT PEOPLE LIKE
us," the woman said. She was a cashier at a filling
station. Her husband was a construction worker.
She added, "Maybe if they lived in a two-bedroom
trailer, it would be different."

Who was she talking about? "They" were the
two candidates for president in 2000. The
Republican candidate was George W. Bush, son of
the man who had been president before Bill
Clinton. The Democratic candidate was Al Gore,
who had been vice president for eight years.

That cashier wasn't the only person who
thought that neither of the two candidates really
cared about her and people like her. Many others
felt the same way. An African American woman
who managed a McDonald's, earning barely more

than the minimum wage, said, "I don't even pay attention to those two, and all my friends say the same. My life won't change."

Almost half the voters in the country would not even go to the polls on Election Day 2000. Many saw no real difference in the candidates. They had no way to know that the candidate who became president would soon have to deal with a national crisis—a terrorist attack on the United States that would start a new cycle of war.

A Close Election

BUSH, THE REPUBLICAN CANDIDATE, WAS known for his close ties to the oil industry. Both candidates, though, had support from big business. Bush and Gore had other things in common, too.

Both candidates favored a large military and the continued use of land mines (even though other nations in the world had banned these deadly devices, which can kill or injure civilians many years after combat ends). Both supported the death penalty and the growth of prisons. Neither of them had a plan for free national health care, or for a big increase in low-cost housing, or for a dramatic change in environmental controls.

There was a third candidate. His name was Ralph Nader, and he was nationally known as a critic of the way large corporations control the American economy. Nader's plan for the nation focused on health care, education, and the environment. But Nader was shut out of the debates between presidential candidates that were broadcast on national television. Without the support of big business, he had to raise money from the small contributions of people who believed in his program.

When Election Day came, it turned out to be the strangest election in American history. Gore received hundreds of thousands more votes than Bush. Under the Constitution, though, presidents aren't elected by the direct vote of the people, sometimes called the popular vote. Instead, each state has a certain number of electors. The electors' votes determine who becomes president.

Twice in American history, in 1876 and 1888, a president had been elected who *wasn't* chosen by the majority of voters. That's because the electors' votes don't always match the popular vote. For example, if 45 percent of the voters in a state voted for candidate A, and 55 percent voted for candidate B, the electoral votes might not be divided between the two candidates. Candidate B might get all the electoral votes.

That's how things work in the state of Florida—and that's what caused a raging argument about the presidential election of 2000. Across the nation, the electoral vote between Gore and Bush was extremely close. It was so close that Florida's electoral votes would decide the election.

But it was not clear whether Gore or Bush had received more votes in Florida. It seemed that many votes had not been counted, especially in districts where a lot of black voters lived. Also, ballots were disqualified on technical grounds, and marks made on ballots by voting machines were not clear.

In short, Florida's popular vote was in doubt. Florida's electoral vote hung in the balance, and so did the presidency. But Bush, the Republican candidate, had an advantage. His brother was governor of Florida, and Florida's secretary of state, Katherine Harris, was also a Republican. Her job gave her the power to certify, or officially declare, who had more votes. She rushed through a recount of some of the ballots and announced that Bush had won the Florida vote. This made Bush the new president.

Democrats appealed to the Florida Supreme Court. The court, which was dominated by Democrats, ordered Harris not to certify a winner until the recount of the popular vote was complete. Harris set a deadline for recounting, and although thousands of votes were still disputed, she declared Bush the winner by 537 votes.

Gore prepared to challenge her decision. He wanted the recount to continue, as the Florida Supreme Court had ordered. To keep this from happening, the Republican Party took the case to the nation's highest court, the U.S. Supreme Court.

Four Supreme Court justices felt that the Florida recount should continue. They argued that the Court did not have the right to interfere with the way the Florida Supreme Court had interpreted its state's electoral law. But the five conservative judges on the court overruled the Florida Supreme Court and halted the recount. In the end, the U.S. Supreme Court's ruling let

Harris's certification stand. Bush got Florida's electoral votes.

John Paul Stevens was one of the liberal justices who had voted not to interfere with the Florida Supreme Court. With some bitterness, he summed up the results of the Court's decision:

> Although we may never know with complete certainty
> the identity of the winner of this year's presidential
> decision, the identity of the loser is perfectly clear. It is
> the nation's confidence in the judge as an impartial
> guardian of the rule of law.

The Terrorist Attack and the Response

NINE MONTHS AFTER BUSH TOOK OFFICE, on September 11, 2001, a terrible event pushed all other issues into the background. Hijackers on three planes flew the huge jets, loaded with fuel, into the twin towers of the World Trade Center in New York City, and into the Pentagon in Washington, D.C.

(right)
The World Trade
Center south tower
bursts into flames,
New York City,
September 11, 2001.

Americans all over the country watched, horrified, as the towers collapsed in an inferno of

concrete and metal. Thousands of people who worked in the towers were buried in the wreckage. So were hundreds of firefighters and police officers who had gone to their rescue.

Nineteen men from the Middle East, most from Saudi Arabia, had made this attack against huge symbols of American wealth and power. They were willing to die to strike a deadly blow against the superpower that they saw as their enemy.

President Bush immediately declared a "war on terrorism." Congress rushed to give the president the power to take military action without the formal declaration of war that the U.S. Constitution requires. Only one member of Congress disagreed—Barbara Lee, an African American representative from California.

The administration believed that the attack was ordered by Osama bin Laden, a Saudi Arabian who supported a militant form of Islam, the Muslim religion. He was thought to be hiding somewhere in the Asian nation of Afghanistan, so Bush ordered the bombing of Afghanistan.

The president set out to capture or kill Osama bin Laden and to destroy his militant Islamic organization, called Al-Qaeda. But after five months of bombing, Osama bin Laden remained free. Bush had to admit to Congress that "tens of thousands of trained terrorists are still at large" in "dozens of countries."

Bush and his advisers should have known that terrorism could not be defeated by force. Evidence from many countries and time periods shows that when countries respond to terrorist acts with military force, the result is more terrorism.

The bombing of Afghanistan was devastating to the country, which had already suffered a 1979 invasion by the Soviet Union, followed by a civil war. Although the Pentagon claimed that the United States was bombing only military targets, human rights groups and the press reported at least a thousand civilians killed. But the mainstream press and major television networks did not show Americans the full extent of the human suffering in Afghanistan. Instead, the media encouraged a mood of revenge.

Congress passed a law called the Patriot Act. It gave the Department of Justice the power to hold noncitizens on nothing more than suspicion, without charging them with a crime, and without the protections guaranteed in the Constitution.

AN EYE FOR AN EYE
LEAVES THE
WHOLE WORLD
BLIND
MBER
T. II VICTIMS

And although President Bush cautioned Americans not to take out their anger on Arab Americans, the government rounded up people for questioning. Most were Muslims. A thousand or more were held without charges.

In the wartime atmosphere, it became hard for citizens to criticize the government's actions. A retired telephone worker was at his health club when he made a remark critical of President Bush. Later he was questioned by the Federal Bureau of Investigation (FBI). A young woman found two FBI agents at her door. They said they had gotten reports of posters on her wall, criticizing the president.

Still, some people spoke out against the war. At peace rallies all over the country, they carried signs with slogans such as "Our Grief Is Not a Cry for Revenge" and "Justice, Not War."

Family members of people who had died in the September 11 attacks wrote to the president. They urged him not to match violence with violence, not to bomb the people of Afghanistan. Amber Amundsen's husband, an Army Specialist, had been killed in the attack on the Pentagon. She wrote:

(*left*) Demonstrators holding signs gather at an anti-war rally in Washington, 2001.

I have heard angry rhetoric [speech] by some Americans, including many of our nation's leaders, who advise a heavy dose of revenge and punishment. To those leaders, I would like to make clear that my family and I take no comfort in your words of rage. If you choose to respond to this incomprehensible brutality by perpetuating [continuing] violence against other innocent human beings, you may not do so in the name of my husband.

Some families of September 11 victims traveled to Afghanistan to meet Afghan families who had lost loved ones in the American bombing. One of the Americans was Rita Lasar, whose brother had died in the attack. Lasar said that she would devote the rest of her life to working for peace.

Critics of the bombing felt that terrorism was rooted in deep complaints against the United States. The way to stop terrorism was to respond to these complaints.

Some of the Islamic world's complaints were easy to identify. The United States had stationed troops in Saudi Arabia, where Islam's holiest shrines are located. For ten years the United States had kept Iraq from trading with other countries—a move that was supposed to be political, but one that had caused the deaths of hundreds of thousands of children by keeping food and medicine out of the country, according to the United Nations. The United States also supported the nation of Israel in its occupation of land claimed by Palestinian Muslims.

To change its position on these matters, the United States would have to withdraw military forces around the world. It would have to give up political and economic power over other countries. In short, America would have to stop being a superpower. This was something that the military-industrial interests of both political parties could not accept.

Three years before September 11, 2001, a former U.S. Air Force officer named Robert Bowman had written about terrorist attacks on American embassies in Africa. He described the roots of terrorism:

> We are not hated because we practice democracy, value freedom, or uphold human rights. We are hated because our government denies these things to people in Third World countries whose resources are coveted [desired] by our multinational corporations. That hatred we have sown has come back to haunt us in the form of terrorism. . . . Instead of sending our sons and daughters around the

world to kill Arabs so we can have the oil under their sand, we should send them to rebuild their infrastructure, supply clean water, and feed starving children. . . .

In short, we should do good instead of evil. Who would try to stop us? Who would hate us? Who would want to bomb us? That is the truth the American people need to hear.

Voices such as Bowman's were mostly shut out of the American media after the September 11 attacks. But there was a chance that their powerful message might spread among the American people, once they saw that meeting violence with violence did not solve the problem of terrorism.

CHAPTER THIRTEEN

WAR IN IRAQ, CONFLICT AT HOME

THE UNITED STATES MADE "WAR ON TERROR" its mission after the September 11, 2001, terrorist attacks on New York City and Washington, D.C. Soon that mission would lead American troops into war in the Middle Eastern nation of Iraq. As voices at home spoke out against the war, the administration of President George W. Bush faced other troubles. A deadly hurricane made people around the world question the U.S. government's commitment to social justice, and debates about immigration made people ask what it means to be an American. In an election in 2006, voters in the United States showed that they were ready for change.

Afghanistan after the U.S. Invasion

WHEN UNITED STATES FORCES BOMBED AND invaded Afghanistan, they failed to capture Osama bin Laden or to destroy the Al-Qaeda organization. Yet the military operation killed thousands of Afghan civilians and forced hundreds of thousands from their homes.

U.S. leaders justified this terrible toll on the grounds that the invasion had removed the Taliban from power.

The Taliban was a fundamentalist Islamic group that had been ruling Afghanistan with an iron hand. Among other things, the Taliban insisted on strict interpretations of Islam that denied rights to women. The defeat of the Taliban brought a group called the Northern Alliance into power. Its record was far from spotless. In the mid-1990s, the Northern Alliance had committed many acts of violence against the people of Kabul and other Afghan cities.

In his 2002 State of the Union Address, Bush claimed that getting rid of the Taliban meant that "women are free" in Afghanistan. This was a false claim, according to an organization of Afghan women. And two years after the U.S. invasion, the

New York Times gave a discouraging account of things in Afghanistan. Women were not free, bandits roamed the land, warlords controlled huge areas, and the Taliban was making a comeback.

Sixteen months into the war, a Scotsman who took medical aid to Afghan villages was distressed at what he saw. He wrote, "The country is on its knees. . . . It is one of the most heavily land-mined countries in the world . . . 25 percent of all children are dead by the age of five." Sadly he concluded, "Surely, at the start of our 21st century, we should have evolved beyond the point where we reduce a country and a people to dust, for the flimsiest of excuses." But as of August 2006, air strikes were still killing Afghan civilians, and the *New York Times* reported widespread "corruption, violence and poverty."

The attack on Afghanistan had not brought democracy or security, and it had not weakened terrorism. If anything, the violence unleashed by the United States had angered people in the Middle East and created more terrorists.

Weapons of Mass Destruction?

WITH AFGHANISTAN STILL IN TURMOIL,
the Bush administration began to set the stage for
a war against Iraq. Richard Clarke, adviser to the
president on terrorism, later said that immediately
after the September 11 attacks the White House
looked for reasons to attack Iraq—even though no
evidence linked Iraq to the attacks.

Bush and the government officials close to him
wanted the American public to think that Iraq and
its dictator, Saddam Hussein, threatened the
United States and the world. They accused Iraq of
concealing "weapons of mass destruction," including plans to build a nuclear bomb.

A United Nations team made hundreds of
inspections all over Iraq. It found no weapons of
mass destruction, or any evidence that Iraq was
working on a nuclear weapon. U.S. vice president
Richard Cheney, though, insisted the weapons
were real. Condoleezza Rice, the secretary of state,
spoke menacingly of "a mushroom cloud," like
the cloud caused by the atomic bombing of
Hiroshima, Japan. The government also pointed
to Hussein's cruel and illegal acts, such as the use
of chemical poisons to massacre five thousand

Iraqis from the Kurdish ethnic minority. But Hussein had killed those Kurds in 1988, and at the time the United States had not objected loudly. Back then, Iraq and the United States had been on the same side against Iran, another nation in the Middle East.

What was the real reason for building up the idea of war against Iraq in 2002? Maybe the reason lay underground. Iraq had the world's second largest oil reserves, after Saudi Arabia. Ever since the end of World War II in 1945, the United States had been determined to control the oil of the Middle East. Oil shaped U.S. decisions about the Middle East during both Democratic and Republican presidencies. The administration of President Jimmy Carter, a liberal Democrat, had produced the "Carter Doctrine." Under this doctrine, the United States claimed the right to defend its interest in Middle Eastern oil "by any means necessary, including military force."

In September 2002, the Bush administration said that it would take military action on Iraq on its own, without the support of other countries. This violated the charter of the United Nations, which allows military action only in self-defense, and only when approved by the U.N. Security Council. Nevertheless, the United States prepared to make war on Iraq. Protests took place all over the world. On February 15, 2003, ten to fifteen million people across the globe demonstrated against the coming war at the same time.

The Iraq War Begins

DESPITE THE PROTESTS, THE UNITED STATES government launched a massive attack on Iraq on March 20, 2003. "Operation Iraqi Freedom," as it was called, dropped thousands of bombs on Iraq and sent more than a hundred thousand soldiers into the country. Hundreds of U.S. soldiers were killed. Thousands of Iraqis died, many of them civilians.

After three weeks, U.S. forces occupied Iraq's capital, Baghdad. After six weeks, major military operations were declared over. President Bush stood triumphantly on a U.S. aircraft carrier, in front of a huge banner that said, "Mission Accomplished."

But the mission to control Iraq wasn't accomplished. Violence grew as Iraqi insurgents attacked the U.S. army. The capture of Saddam Hussein in December 2003 did nothing to stop the attacks.

Iraqis grew more and more resentful of the U.S. occupation of their country. American troops rounded up Iraqis suspected of being insurgents. Thousands of Iraqis were held prisoner. When photos appeared showing U.S. troops torturing Iraqi prisoners, there was evidence that this behavior had the approval of the U.S. secretary of defense. All of these things fed the fire of Iraqi hostility toward the United States. Polls showed that a vast majority of the Iraqis wanted U.S. troops out of Iraq.

The Bush administration refused to consider withdrawing from Iraq. Meanwhile, U.S. casualties were mounting. By the middle of 2006, more than 2,500 Americans had died. Thousands more were wounded, often quite severely. The administration went to great lengths to keep the American public from seeing the coffins, and to keep the armless and legless veterans out of sight.

As bad as American casualties were, Iraqi casualties were much greater. By mid-2006, hundreds of thousands of Iraqis had died. The country was a shambles. People lacked clean water and electricity and lived amid violence and chaos.

At the beginning of the war, a large majority of the American people had accepted the Bush administration's argument that Saddam Hussein had "weapons of mass destruction," and that the invasion of Iraq was part of the "war on terror." The major media did not question this, and the Democratic Party largely supported the war.

But as the war went on, the situation became clearer. Operation Iraqi Freedom had brought neither democracy, nor freedom, nor security to Iraq. The U.S. government had deceived the American people about "weapons of mass destruction" that did not exist. It had claimed that the attacks of September 11, 2001, were linked to Iraq, when there was no evidence to show this. It had supported torture and imprisonment without trial for thousands of people in Iraq and in the United States.

The administration was also using the war as an excuse for violating Americans' constitutional rights. Under the Patriot Act, the United States could pick up people in Afghanistan and other places and accuse them of terrorism. Instead of treating them as prisoners of war, who have rights under international law, the government created a new label for them: "unlawful enemy combatants." They were locked up in Guantánamo Bay, a U.S. military installation in Cuba. Rumors of torture came out of this prison, and some prisoners committed suicide.

In the fall of 2006, the U.S. Congress passed a bill that allowed the Central Intelligence Agency (CIA) to continue the harsh interrogation of suspected terrorists in secret prisons around the world. The bill also did away with the right of habeas corpus for an "unlawful enemy combatant," even a U.S. citizen. The loss of this right, which is guaranteed in the U.S. Constitution's Bill of Rights, meant that prisoners would not be brought before a court to challenge their arrest.

The Anti-War Movement

PROTESTS AGAINST THE WAR IN IRAQ TOOK place all over the United States. They were smaller than the huge anti-war demonstrations of the Vietnam era, but they showed that the Bush administration's policies were losing support.

Cindy Sheehan, whose son Casey died in Iraq, spoke out powerfully against the war. When she camped near Bush's ranch in Crawford, Texas, she drew support from all over the country. In a speech to a Veterans for Peace gathering in Dallas, Sheehan addressed President Bush: "You tell me the truth. You tell me that my son died for oil."

As the war in Iraq continued, young people who had joined the military began to reconsider. Diedra Cobb of Illinois declared herself a conscientious objector, someone whose moral beliefs prevent her from fighting. Cobb wrote, "I joined the Army thinking that I was, quite possibly, upholding some of the mightiest of ideals for the greatest, most powerful country on this earth. . . . There had to be some good that would come out of the carnage, in the end. But this is where I made my mistake, because in war there is no end."

(left)
Anti-war activist Cindy Sheehan speaks to the news media at the White House, 2005.

Between the beginning of the war and the end of 2004, according to CBS news, 5,500 soldiers deserted. Many went to Canada. One of them was a former staff sergeant in the Marine Corps. He told a hearing in Toronto that he and his fellow marines shot and killed more than thirty unarmed men, women, and children, including a young Iraqi who got out of his car with his arms in the air.

An English newspaper, *The Independent,* reported on U.S. deserters. It said, "Sergeant Kevin Benderman cannot shake the images from his head. There are bombed villages and desperate people. There are dogs eating corpses thrown into a mass grave. And most unremitting of all, there is the image of a young Iraqi girl, no more than eight or nine, one arm severely burnt and blistered, and the sound of her screams."

It was getting harder to get young Americans to join the armed forces, so the military stepped up its recruiting efforts. Recruiters targeted teenagers. They visited high schools, approaching students at football games and in school cafeterias. Anti-war groups took up the challenge. They visited schools to tell young people the other side of the story.

By 2006, polls showed that a majority of Americans were against the war and lacked confidence in President Bush. Some journalists began to speak out boldly, even in media that earlier had supported the administration or remained quiet. On Memorial Day, May 30, Andy Rooney told viewers of the television show *60 Minutes* that he was a veteran of World War II. Then he said, "We use the phrase 'gave their lives,' but they didn't give their lives. Their lives were taken from them. . . . I wish we could dedicate Memorial Day, not to the memory of those who have died at war, but to the idea of saving the lives of the young people who are going to die in the future if we don't find some new way— some new religion maybe—that takes war out of our lives."

Salt Lake City, Utah, is generally considered a conservative place, one that would support the administration's war in Iraq. But thousands of people cheered Mayor "Rocky" Anderson when he called President Bush a "dishonest, war-mongering, human-rights violating president." Bush's time in office, declared Anderson, would "rank as the worst presidency our nation has ever had to endure."

Two Storms

THE BUSH ADMINISTRATION TRIED HARD TO
keep the country in a fiercely nationalistic mood—
a mood of "us versus them" that would whip up
support for the Iraq war and other administration
policies. One result of this strong nationalist feeling was a wave of resentment against millions of
immigrants, especially Mexicans, who had come
to the United States without legal status. These
immigrants were seen as taking jobs from people
in the United States, even though various studies
showed that they did not hurt the economy, but
helped it.

Congress approved plans to build a 750–mile
fence along the southern borders of California and
Arizona. It was supposed to keep out Mexicans who
were trying to escape the poverty in their home
country. The U.S. government did not seem to see
the irony in the idea of a fence to keep poor
Mexicans from coming *into* territory that the United
States had seized from Mexico in the 1840s.

In the spring of 2005, Congress discussed laws
to punish people who were in the United States
illegally. Huge demonstrations took place around
the country, especially in California and the

(left)
Protesters
holding a massive
American flag
during the
immigration rally
in downtown
Dallas, 2006.

Southwest, as hundreds of thousands of people demanded equal rights for immigrants. The protestors included both immigrants and Americans who supported them. One of their slogans was "No Human Being Is Illegal."

The Bush administration faced growing disapproval of the war in Iraq and criticism of its immigration policy at home. Then a natural disaster struck. In August 2005, Hurricane Katrina hit the Gulf Coast states of Mississippi and Louisiana. The levees that protected the city of New Orleans from the Mississippi River gave way. Together, the storm and flood destroyed much of the city, killed or injured thousands of people, and left hundreds of thousands homeless.

Americans and the world were shocked when the federal government was slow and inefficient in helping survivors in the stricken city. "People around the world cannot believe what they're seeing," said an article in the *Washington Post*. "From Argentina to Zimbabwe, front-page photos of the dead and desperate in New Orleans, almost all of them poor and black, have sickened them, and shaken assumptions about American might. How can this be happening, they ask, in a nation whose

wealth and power seem almost supernatural in so
many struggling corners of the world. . .
International reaction has shifted in many cases
from shock, sympathy and generosity to a growing
criticism of the Bush administration's response to
the catastrophe of Hurricane Katrina."

The Katrina experience also reminded people
that while millions in Africa, in Asia, and even in
the Untied States were dying of malnutrition and
sickness, and while natural disasters were taking
huge tolls of life all over the world, the United
States government was pouring its enormous
wealth into war and the building of empire.

In November of 2006, Americans went to the
polls to elect members of the House of
Representatives and the Senate. The voters had
many issues on their minds. One of the most important must have been the disastrous war in Iraq, and
the way it was draining the nation's wealth.

When the votes were counted, the Democratic
Party had taken control from the Republicans in
both the House of Representatives and the Senate by
a narrow margin. This didn't mean that Americans
were filled with enthusiasm for the Democrats, but
it did mean that they were saying "no" to the admin-

istration of George W. Bush, the Republican president. The voters had taken the power of government away from the president's party, and they had given politicians a chance to lead the country in a new direction. It was a rare democratic moment in the recent history of the nation.

CHAPTER FOURTEEN

"RISE LIKE LIONS"

I AM OFTEN ASKED HOW I CAME TO WRITE
this book. One reason is that after twenty years of
teaching history and political science, I wanted to
write a different kind of history book—one that
was different from the ones I had had in school,
and the ones given to students across the country.

By that time, I knew that there is no such thing
as a pure fact. Behind every fact that a teacher or
writer presents to the world is a judgment. The
judgment says, "This fact is important, and other
facts, which I am leaving out, are not important." I
thought that some of the things that had been left
out of most history books were important.

The beginning of the Declaration of
Independence says that "We the people" wrote
the document. But the authors of the Declaration

were really fifty-five privileged white men. They belonged to a class that wanted a strong central government to protect their interests. Right down to this day, government has been used to serve the needs of the wealthy and powerful. This fact is hidden by language that suggests that all of us—rich and poor and middle class—want the same thing.

Race is another issue. I did not realize, when I first started to study history, how badly twisted the teaching and writing of history had become by ignoring nonwhite people. Yes, the Indians were there, and then they were gone. Black people were visible when they were slaves, then they were freed, and they became invisible. It was a white man's history. Massacres of Indians and of black people got little attention, if they were mentioned at all.

Other themes and issues were also overlooked in the standard, mainstream telling of history. The suffering of the poor did not get much attention. Wars were plentiful, but histories did not tell us much about the men and women and children on all sides who were killed or crippled when leaders made the decision to go to war. The struggles for justice by Latino people in California and the Southwest were often ignored. So were the claims of gay and lesbian people for their rights, and the change in the national culture that they brought about.

The title of this book is not quite accurate. A "people's history" promises more than any one person can deliver, and it is the hardest kind of history to recapture. I call it that anyway because, with all its limits, it is a history that is disrespectful of governments and respectful of people's movements of resistance.

Most history books suggest that in times of crisis we must look to someone to save us. In the Revolutionary crisis, the Founding Fathers saved us. In the Civil War, Lincoln saved us. In the Depression, Franklin D. Roosevelt saved us. Our role is just to go to voting booths every four years. But from time to time, Americans reject the idea of a savior. They feel their own strength, and they rebel.

So far, their rebellions have been contained. The Establishment—the club of business leaders, generals, and politicians—has always managed to keep up the pretense of national unity, with a government that claims to represent all the people. But the Establishment would like Americans to forget the times when people who seemed helpless were able to resist, and people who seemed content demanded change. Blacks, women, Indians, young people, working people—all have found ways to make their voices heard, and to bring about change.

Most histories say little about revolt. They place the emphasis on the acts of leaders, not the actions of ordinary citizens. But history that keeps alive the memory of people's resistance suggests new kinds of power.

Imagine the American people united for the first time in a movement for fundamental change. Imagine society's power taken away from the giant corporations, the military, and the politicians who answer to corporate and military interests.

We would need to rebuild the economy for efficiency and justice. We would start on our neighborhoods, cities, and workplaces. Work would be found for everyone. Society would benefit from the enormous energy, skill, and talent that is now unused. The basics—food, housing, health care, education, transportation—would be available to all.

The great problem would be to bring about all this change through cooperation, not through systems of reward and punishment. Social movements of the past give hints of how people might behave if they were working together to build a new society. Decisions would be made by small groups of people, working as equals. Perhaps a new, diverse, nonviolent culture would develop over time. The values of cooperation and freedom would shape people's relationships with one another and the raising of their children.

All of this takes us far from history, into the realm of imagination. But it is not totally removed from history. There are glimpses of such possibilities in the past—in the labor movement, for example, or the Freedom Rides, or the cultural changes of the 1960s and 1970s.

Two forces are now rushing toward the future. One wears a splendid uniform. It is the "official" past, with all its violence, war, prejudices against those who are different, hoarding of the good earth's wealth by the few, and political power in the hands of liars and murderers.

The other force is ragged but inspired. It is the "people's" past, with its history of resistance, civil disobedience against the military machine, protests against racism, multiculturalism, and growing anger against endless wars.

Which of these forces will win the future? It is a race we can all choose to join, or just to watch. But we should know that our choice will help determine the outcome.

Women garment workers in New York City, at the start of the twentieth century, gained inspiration for their own movement of resistance from the words of the poet Shelley:

> Rise like lions after slumber
> In unvanquishable number!
> Shake your chains to earth, like dew
> Which in sleep had fallen on you—
> Ye are many, they are few!

Glossary

Abolitionism Movement to abolish, or end, something, such as slavery

Anarchism A belief that governments are by nature oppressive, and that people should live free from the authority of the state, the church, and corporate power, and share the wealth of the earth

Annex To take control of a territory and add it to a country

Capitalism Economic system in which income-producing property (such as farms and factories) is owned by individuals or corporations and competititon in a free marketplace determines how goods and services will be distributed and priced

Communism The idea that capitalism has outlived its usefulness, that it must be replaced by a system in which the economy is collectively managed, and its wealth distributed according to people's needs

Conservative Tending to support established institutions and traditional values and to be wary of social change

Democracy Government that is ruled by the people, who usually elect representatives to form the government

Depression A period of low economic activity and high unemployment

Elite A group that is powerful within a society, often because of having money, or herditary authority, or noble status

Emigrant Someone who leaves his or her home country to live in a different country

Federalist Supporter of a strong central, or federal, authority; supporter of national interests over states' rights

Feminism The belief that women are equal to men and deserve equal rights

Immigrant Someone who comes into a country to live there

Imperialism Empire building

Indenture A contract that binds a person to work for someone else for a certain length of time

Left-wing **Liberal** or radical

Liberal Tending to support strong civil liberties and to be open to social change

Massacre Killing a number of people, usually in a brutal or violent way

Militia Citizens who are armed and can act as soldiers in an emergency

Monopoly An economic situation in which an entire industry is controlled by a single corporation, or just a few of them

Nationalism Strong loyalty to one's country or ethnic group, with the feeling that that country or group is more important than others, or has higher standing, and that its interests should always be supported

Racism The belief that racial differences make some people better or worse than others; also, treating people differently because of race

Radical Extremely critical of the existing social system

Ratification The process by which something is voted on, accepted, and made into law

Right-wing Politically **conservative**

Socialism A society of equality, in which not profit but usefulness determines what is produced

Speculator Someone who buys large amounts of land, not to use it but to resell it at a profit

Strike An action by people in a **union** who refuse to work until their demands are met

Suffrage The right to vote

Terrorism Acts of violence, possibly against civilians, carried out for political reasons by people who do not formally represent a state or its armed forces

Union Association of workers who bargain for wages and benefits together instead of one by one

Index

Page numbers in *italics* refer to illustrations.

Page numbers in **bold** refer to glossary definitions.

torture
  employed by U.S. military,
    197-198
  trade union movement. *See*
    labor movement
Triangle Shirtwaist Company
  1909 strike, 4
  1911 fire, 5, *8-9*
  Truman, Harry S., 64-66
  launches search for "disloyal
    persons," 67
  and race relations, 73, 75
  "trust-busting," 15

U.S. Constitution, 14, 109, 184
  contravened by Patriot Act,
    185, 198-199
  First Amendment, 25
U.S. Department of Agriculture
  suggests no free second help-
    ings of milk, 139
U.S. Department of Justice, 27,
  30
U.S. government. *See* government
U.S. Post Office
  denies mailing privileges to
    antiwar papers, 26
U.S. Steel Company, 6
unemployment, 41, 139-140, 143
  insurance, 50
  survived by bootlegging coal
    miners, 46-47
union movement. *See* labor
  movement
United Nations, 66, 137, 195-196
  notes ill effects of embargo on
    Iraq, 188-189
upper class. *See* rich people

Vanzetti, Bartolomeo, 32-33
veterans
  advocate draftees to "use their

  own conscience," 157
  protest in Washington, 44-45
  speak of lives taken, 203
Viet Cong, 92, 95-96
Vietnam
  Japanese occupation, 90
  French control and bombing,
    90-91
  partition into North and
    South, 92
  U.S. intervention and secret
    war, 90-93
Vietnam War, 89-103, 157
  blacks and, 97-98
  effect on public opinion of
    government, 121
  Martin Luther King speaks
    out against, 85-86, 98-99
  My Lai massacre, 96
  U.S. bombing of Laos and
    Cambodia, 96-97
  veterans, 99, *100,* 101, 114
violence against blacks, 76, 84,
  87. *See also* lynchings
violence against civil rights
  demonstrators and workers,
    80-82
voting, 177-178, 207-208, 211
  black registration, 81-83
  choice between Tweedledum
    and Tweedledee, 12
  reform, 14
  women gain right to vote, 39
Voting Rights Act, 82
WTO. *See* World Trade
  Organization
Waco, Texas, 166
war
  boosts economy, 63-64
  controls citizens, 64
  makes citizens evacuate
    homes, 94
  protects interests of capital-
    ists, 1
  starts under pretext, 93, 145

HOWARD ZINN is professor emeritus at Boston University. He is the author of the classic *A People's History of the United States*, "a brilliant and moving history of the American people from the point of view of those whose plight has been largely omitted from most histories" (*Library Journal*). The book has now sold more than one million copies.

Zinn has received the Lannan Foundation Literary Award for Nonfiction and the Eugene V. Debs award for his writing and political activism, and in 2003 was awarded the Prix des amis du Monde Diplomatique.

Zinn is the author of numerous books, including *A Power Governments Cannot Suppress*, *Voices of A People's History of the United States* (with Aınthony Arnove), *The Zinn Reader*, the autobiographical *You Can't Be Neutral on a Moving Train*, and the play *Marx in Soho*.

Zinn grew up in Brooklyn and worked in the shipyards before serving as an air force bombardier in World War II. Zinn was chair of the History Department at Spelman College, where he actively participated in the Civil Rights Movement, before taking a position at Boston University.

While there he became a leader in the movement to end the war in Vietnam.

He now lives with his wife, Roslyn, in Massachusetts and lectures widely on history, contemporary politics, and against war.

REBECCA STEFOFF is the author of many books for children and young adults. In addition to writing on a number of topics in American history, including a biography of the Shawnee chieftain Tecumseh and a ten-volume series of historical atlases, she has adapted Ronald Takaki's award-winning history of Asian Americans, *Strangers from a Different Shore,* into a series for young readers. Stefoff received her B.A. from Indiana University and her M.A. from the University of Pennsylvania. Currently she lives in Portland, Oregon.

About the Publisher

SEVEN STORIES PRESS is an independent book publisher based in New York City, with distribution throughout the United States, Canada, England, and Australia. We publish works of the imagination by such writers as Nelson Algren, Octavia E. Butler, Assia Djebar, Ariel Dorfman, Barry Gifford, Lee Stringer, and Kurt Vonnegut, to name a few, together with political titles by voices of conscience, including the Boston Women's Health Book Collective, Noam Chomsky, Ralph Nader, Gary Null, Project Censored, Barbara Seaman, Gary Webb, and Howard Zinn, among many others. Our books appear in hardcover, paperback, pamphlet, and e-book formats, in English and in Spanish. We believe publishers have a special responsibility to defend free speech and human rights, and to celebrate the gifts of the human imagination, wherever we can.

For more information about us, visit our Web site at www.sevenstories.com or write for a free catalogue to Seven Stories Press, 140 Watts Street, New York, NY 10013.